Philoktetes

ALSO BY JAMES SCULLY

Modern Poetics, ed. (McGraw-Hill) / *Modern Poets on Modern Poetry*, ed.
(Wm. Collins, Ltd.)

The Marches (Holt, Rinehart & Winston)

Avenue of the Americas (University of Massachusetts Press)

Santiago Poems (Curbstone Press)

Aeschylus' Prometheus Bound,
co-translated with C. John Herington (Oxford University Press)

Quechua Peoples Poetry,
co-translated with Maria A. Proser (Curbstone Press)

Scrap Book (Ziesling Brothers)

De Repente / All of a Sudden by Teresa de Jesùs,
co-translated with Maria A. Proser and Arlene Scully

May Day (Minnesota Review Press)

Apollo Helmet (Curbstone Press)

Line Break: Poetry as Social Practice
(Bay Press, Curbstone Press, Northwestern University Press)

Raging Beauty: Selected Poems (Azul Editions)

Donatello's Version (Curbstone Press)

Oceania (Azul Editions)

Vagabond Flags journal (Azul Editions)

Angel in Flames: Selected Poems & Translations
(Smokestack Books, UK)

The Complete Plays of Sophocles with Robert Bagg
(Harper Perennial)

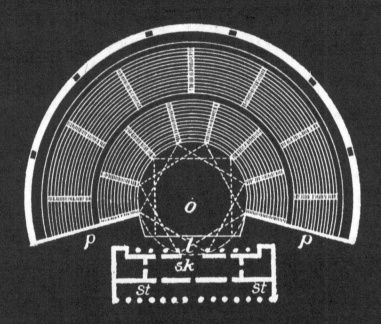

PHILOKTETES

A New Translation by James Scully

SOPHOCLES

HARPER  PERENNIAL

NEW YORK • LONDON • TORONTO • SYDNEY • NEW DELHI • AUCKLAND

HARPER ● PERENNIAL

For performance rights to *Philoktetes* contact The Strothman Agency, LLC, at 197 Eighth Street, Flagship Wharf – 611, Charlestown, MA 02129, or by email at info@strothmanagency.com.

HarperCollins books may be purchased for educational, business, or sales promotional use. For information please write: Special Markets Department, HarperCollins Publishers, 10 East 53rd Street, New York, NY 10022.

FIRST EDITION

Designed by Justin Dodd

Library of Congress Cataloging-in-Publication Data is available upon request.

ISBN 978-0-06-213216-1

12 13 14 15 16   /RRD   10 9 8 7 6 5 4 3 2 1

For the many teachers and interpreters who have held to,
and communicated, the living historicity of these plays

CONTENTS

CONTENTS

WHEN THEATER WAS LIFE: THE WORLD OF SOPHOCLES

I

Greek theater emerged from the same explosive creativity that propelled the institutions and ways of knowing of ancient Athens, through two and a half millennia, into our own era. These ranged from the concept and practice of democracy, to an aggressive use of logic with few holds barred, to a philosophy singing not of gods and heroes but of what exists, where it came from, and why. Athenians distinguished history from myth, acutely observed the human form, and reconceived medicine from a set of beliefs and untheorized practices into a science.

Playwrights, whose work was presented to audiences of thousands, effectively took center stage as critics and interpreters of their own culture. Athenian drama had one major showing each year at the nine-day Festival of Dionysos. It was rigorously vetted. Eight dramatists (three tragedians, five comic playwrights), chosen in open competition, were "granted choruses," a down-to-earth term meaning that the city financed production of their plays. For the Athenians theater was as central to civic life as the assembly, law courts, temples, and agora.

Historians summing up Athens' cultural importance have tended to emphasize its glories, attending less to the brutal institutions and policies that underwrote the city's wealth and dominance: its slaves, for instance, who worked the mines that enriched the communal treasury; or its policy of executing the men and enslaving the women and children of enemy cities that refused to surrender on demand. During its long war with Sparta, Athens' raw and unbridled democracy became increasingly reckless, cruel, and eventually self-defeating. Outside the assembly's daily debates on war, peace, and myriad other issues, Athenian citizens, most notably the indefatigable Socrates, waged ongoing critiques of the city's actions and principles. Playwrights, whom the Athenians called *didaskaloi* (educators), were expected to enlighten audiences about themselves, both individually and collectively. As evidenced by the thirty-three plays that survive, these works presented a huge audience annually with conflicts and dilemmas of the most extreme sort.

To some extent all Sophocles' plays engage personal, social, and political crises and confrontations—not just those preserved in heroic legend but those taking place in his immediate world. Other Athenian intellectuals, including Thucydides, Aeschylus, Euripides, Plato, and Aristophanes, were part of that open-ended discussion in which everything was subject to question, including the viability of the city and its democracy (which was twice voted temporarily out of existence).

II

To this day virtually every Athenian theatrical innovation—from paraphernalia such as scenery, costumes, and masks to the architecture of stage and seating and, not least, to the use of drama as a powerful means of cultural and political commentary—remains in use. We thus inherit from Athens the vital *potential* for drama to engage our realities and to support or critique prevailing orthodoxies.

The myths that engaged Sophocles' audience originated in Homer's epics of the Trojan War and its aftermath. Yet Homer's world was tribal. That of the Greek tragedians was not, or only nominally so. With few exceptions (e.g., Aeschylus' *The Persians*), those playwrights were writing *through* the Homeric world to address, and deal with, the *polis* world they themselves were living in. Sophocles was appropriating stories and situations from these epics, which were central to the mythos of Athenian culture, and re-visioning them into dramatic *agons* (contests) relevant to the tumultuous, often vicious politics of Greek life in the fifth century BCE. Today some of Sophocles' concerns, and the way he approached them, correspond at their deepest levels to events and patterns of thought and conduct that trouble our own time. For example, "[Sophocles'] was an age when war was endemic. And Athens in the late fifth century BC appeared to have a heightened taste for conflict. One year of two in the Democratic Assembly, Athenian citizens voted in favor of military aggression" (Hughes, 138).

Each generation interprets and translates these plays in keeping with the style and idiom it believes best suited for tragedy.

Inevitably even the most skilled at preserving the original's essentials, while attuning its voice to the present, will eventually seem the relic of a bygone age. We have assumed that a contemporary translation should attempt to convey not only what the original seems to have been communicating, but *how* it communicated—not in its saying, only, but in its *doing*. It cannot be said too often: these plays were social and historical *events* witnessed by thousands in a context and setting infused with religious ritual and civic protocol. They were not transitory, one-off entertainments but were preserved, memorized, and invoked. Respecting this basic circumstance will not guarantee a successful translation, but it is a precondition for giving these works breathing room in which their strangeness, their rootedness in distinct historical moments, can flourish. As with life itself, they were not made of words alone.

Athenian playwrights relied on a settled progression of scene types: usually a prologue followed by conversations or exchanges in which situations and attitudes are introduced, then a series of confrontations that feature cut-and-thrust dialogue interrupted by messenger narratives, communal songs of exultation or grieving, and less emotionally saturated, or 'objective,' choral odes that respond to or glance off the action. Audiences expected chorus members to be capable of conveying the extraordinary range of expressive modes, from the pithy to the operatic, that Sophocles had at his disposal. To translate this we have needed the resources not only of idiomatic English but also of rhetorical gravitas and, on occasion, colloquial English. Which is why we have adopted, regarding vocabulary and 'levels of speech,' a wide and varied palette. When Philoktetes exclaims, "You said it, boy," that saying corresponds in character to the colloquial Greek expression. On the other hand Aias's "Long rolling waves of time . . ." is as elevated, without being pompous, as anything can be.

Unfortunately we've been taught, and have learned to live with, washed-out stereotypes of the life and art of 'classical' times—just as we have come to associate Greek sculpture with the color of its underlying material, usually white marble. The classical historian Bettany Hughes writes in *The Hemlock Cup* (81) that temples and monuments were painted or stained in "Technicolor" to be seen under the bright Attic sun. The statues' eyes were not blanks gazing off into space. They had color: a *look*. To restore their flesh tones, their eye color, and the bright hues of their cloaks would seem a desecration. We should understand that this is so—even as we recognize that, for us, there is no going back. We've been conditioned to preserve not the reality of ancient Greek sculpture in its robust cultural ambience and physical setting, but our own fixed conception of it as colorless and sedate—a perception created, ironically, by the weathering and ravages of centuries. No one can change that. Still, as translators we have a responsibility not to reissue a stereotype of classical Greek culture but rather to recoup, to the extent possible, the vitality of its once living reality.

Regarding its highly inflected language, so different from our more context-driven modern English, we recognize that locutions sounding contorted, coy, recondite, or annoyingly roundabout were a feature of ordinary Greek and were intensified in theatrical discourse. Highly wrought, larger-than-life expressions, delivered without artificial amplification to an audience of thousands, did not jar when resonating in the vast Theater of Dionysos, but may to our own Anglophone ears when delivered from our more intimate stages and screens, or read in our books and electronic tablets. Accordingly, where appropriate, and especially in rapid exchanges, we have our characters speak more straightforwardly—as happens in Greek stichomythia, when characters argue back and forth in alternating lines (or 'rows') of verse, usually linked by a word they hold in common. Here, for example, is a snippet from *Aias* (1305–1309)[1] that pivots on "right," "killer," "dead" and "god(s)":

TEUKROS   A righteous cause is my courage.
MENELAOS What? It's right to defend my killer?
TEUKROS   Your killer!? You're dead? And still alive?
MENELAOS A god saved me. But he *wanted* me dead.
TEUKROS   If the gods saved you, why disrespect them?

There are no rules for determining when a more-literal or less-literal approach is appropriate. Historical and dramatic context have to be taken into account. The objective is not only to render the textual meaning (which is ordinarily more on the phrase-by-phrase than the word-by-word level) but also to communicate the feel and impact embedded in that meaning. Dictionaries are indispensable for translators, but they are not sufficient. The meanings of words are immeasurably more nuanced and wide-ranging in life than they can ever be in a lexicon. As in life, where most 'sayings' cannot be fully grasped apart from their timing and their place in both personal and social contexts, so in theater: dramatic context must take words up and finish them off. In *Aias*, Teukros, the out-of-wedlock half brother of Aias, and Menelaos, co-commander of the Greek forces, are trading insults. When Menelaos says, "The archer, far from blood dust, thinks he's something," Teukros quietly rejoins, "I'm very good at what I do" (1300–1301).

Understanding the exchange between the two men requires that the reader or audience recognize the 'class' implications of archery. Socially and militarily, archers rank low in the pecking order. They stand to the rear of the battle formation. Archers are archers usually because they can't afford the armor one needs to be a hoplite, a frontline fighter. The point is that Teukros refuses to accept 'his place' in the social and military order. For a Greek audience, the sheer fact of standing his ground against a commander had to have been audacious. But that is not how it automatically registers in most modern word-by-word translations, which tend to make Teukros sound defensive (a trait wholly out of his character in this play). Examples: (a) "Even so, 'tis no sordid craft that I possess," (b) "I'm not the master of a menial skill," (c) "My archery is no contemptible science," (d) "The art I practice is no mean one." These translations are technically accurate. They're scrupulous in reproducing the Greek construction whereby, in an idiomatic context, a negative may register as an assertion—or even, framed as a negative future question, become a command. But tonally, in modern English idiom, Teukros' negation undercuts his assertion (the 'I'm not . . . but even so' formula). To our ears it admits weakness or defensiveness. "I'm very good at what I do," however, is a barely veiled threat. The dramatic arc of the encounter, which confirms that Teukros will not back down for anything or anyone, not even a commander of the Greek army, substantiates that Sophocles meant it to be heard as such.

Hearing the line in context we realize instantly not only what the words are saying but, more pointedly and feelingly, what they're doing. His words are not just 'about' something. They are an act in themselves—not, as in the more literal translations, a duress-driven apologia. Translation must thus respond to an individual character's ever-changing demeanor and circumstance. The speaker's state of mind should show through his or her words, just as in life. Idiomatic or colloquial expressions fit many situations better—especially those that have a more finely tuned emotional economy—than phrases that, if uninhabited, hollowed out, or just plain buttoned-up, sound evasive or euphemistic. Many of the speeches Sophocles gives his characters are as abrupt and common as he might himself have spoken to his fellow Athenians in the assembly, in the agora, to his troops, his actors, or his family.

At times we have chosen a more literal translation in passages where scholars have opted for a seemingly more accessible modern phrase. At the climactic moment in *Oedipus the King*, when Oedipus realizes he has killed his father and fathered children with his mother, he says in a modern prose version by Hugh Lloyd-Jones: "Oh, oh! All is now clear. O light, may I now look on you for the last time, I who am revealed as cursed in my birth, cursed in my marriage, cursed in my killing!" (Greek 1182–1885). When Lloyd-Jones uses and repeats the word "cursed," he is compressing a longer Greek phrase meaning "being shown to have done what must not be done." This compression shifts the emphasis from his unsuspecting human actions toward the realm of the god who acted to "curse" him. The following lines keep the original grammatical construction:

> All! All! It has all happened!
> It was all true. O light! Let this
> be the last time I look on you.
> You see now who I am—
> the child who must not be born!
> I loved where I must not love!
> I killed where I must not kill! (1336–1342)

Here Oedipus names the three acts of interfamilial transgression that it was both his good and his ill fortune to have survived, participated in, and inflicted—birth, sexual love, and murder in self-defense—focusing not only on the curse each act has become but now realizing the full and horrific consequence of each action that was, as it happened, unknowable. Registering the shudder rushing through him, Oedipus's exclamations convey the shock of his realization: *I did these things without feeling their horror as I do now.*

Finally, translations tend to be more or less effective depending on their ability to convey the emotional and physiological reactions that will give a reader or an audience a kinesthetic relationship to the dramatic moment, whether realized as text or performance. This is a precondition for maintaining the tactility that characterizes any living language. Dante wrote that the spirit of poetry abounds "in the tangled constructions and defective pronunciations" of vernacular speech where language is renewed and transformed. We have not attempted that—these are translations, not new works—but we have striven for a language that is spontaneous and generative as opposed to one that is studied and bodiless. We have also worked to preserve the root meaning of Sophocles' Greek, especially his always illuminating metaphors.

III

Sophocles reveals several recurrent attitudes in his plays—sympathy for fate's victims, hostility toward leaders who abuse their power, skepticism toward self-indulgent 'heroes,' disillusionment with war and revenge—that are both personal and politically significant. All his plays to a greater or lesser degree focus on outcasts from their communities. Historically, those who transgress a community's values have either been physically exiled or stigmatized by sanctions and/or shunning. To keep a polity from breaking apart, everyone, regardless of social standing, must abide by certain enforceable communal expectations. Athens in the fifth century BCE practiced political ostracism, a procedure incorporated in its laws. By voting to ostracize a citizen, Athens withdrew its protection and civic benefits—sometimes to punish an offender, but also as a kind of referee's move, expelling a divisive public figure from the city (and from his antagonists) so as to promote a ten-year period of relative peace.

In earlier eras Greek cities also cast out those who committed sacrilege. Murderers of kin, for instance, or blasphemers of a god—in myth and in real life—were banished from Greek cities until the 'unclean' individual 'purged' his crime according to current religious custom. The imperative to banish a kin violator runs so deep that Oedipus, after discovering he has committed patricide and incest, passes judgment on himself, and demands to live in exile. In *Oedipus at Kolonos*, he and Antigone have been exiled from Thebes against their will. In the non-Oedipus plays, the title characters Philoktetes, Elektra, and Aias, as well as Herakles in *Women of Trakhis*, are not outcasts in the traditional sense, though all have actively or involuntarily offended their social units in some way. They may or may not be typical tragic characters; nonetheless none 'fit' the world they're given to live in. In these translations we've incorporated awareness of social dimensions in the original texts, which, as they involve exercises of power, are no less political than social.

In each of the four non-Oedipus plays, a lethal confrontation or conflict 'crazes' the surface coherence of a society (presumed to be Athenian society, either in itself or as mediated through a military context), thus revealing and heightening its internal contradictions.

In *Women of Trakhis* the revered hero Herakles, when he tries to impose a young concubine on his wife Deianeira, provokes her to desperate measures that unwittingly cause him horrific pain, whereupon he exposes his savage and egomaniacal nature, lashing out at everyone around him, exercising a hero's prerogatives so savagely that he darkens his own reputation and drives his wife to suicide and his son to bitter resentment.

Elektra exposes the dehumanizing cost of taking revenge, by revealing the neurotic, materialistic, and cold-blooded character of the avengers. In *Aias*, when the Greek Army's most powerful soldier tries to assassinate his commanders, whose authority rests on dubious grounds, he exposes not only them but his own growing obsolescence in a prolonged war that has more need of strategic acumen, as exemplified by Odysseus, than brute force. In *Philoktetes* the title character, abandoned on a deserted island because of a stinking wound his fellow warriors can't live with, is recalled to active service with the promise of a cure and rehabilitation. The army needs him and his bow to win the war. It is a call he resists, until the god Herakles negotiates a resolution—not in the name of justice, but because Philoktetes' compliance is culturally mandated. As in *Aias*, the object is to maintain the integrity and thus the survival of the society itself. The greatest threat is not an individual's death, which here is not the preeminent concern, but the disintegration of a society.

In our own time aspects of *Aias* and *Philoktetes* have been used for purposes that Sophocles, who was the sponsor in Athens of a healing cult, might have appreciated. Both heroes, but especially Aias, have been appropriated as exemplars of post-traumatic stress disorder, in particular as suffered by soldiers in and out of a war zone. Excerpts from these two plays have been performed around the United States for veterans, soldiers on active duty, their families, and concerned others. Ultimately, however, Sophocles is intent on engaging and resolving internal contradictions that threaten the historical continuity, the very future, of the Athenian city-state. He invokes the class contradictions Athens was experiencing by applying them to the mythical/historical eras from which he draws his plots.

Modern-day relevancies implicit in Sophocles' plays will come sharply into focus or recede from view depending on time and circumstance. The constant factors in these plays will always be their consummate poetry, dramatic propulsion, and the intensity with which they illuminate human motivation and morality. Scholars have also identified allusions in his plays to events in Athenian history. The plague in *Oedipus the King* is described in detail so vivid it dovetails in many respects with Thucydides' more clinical account of the plague that killed one-third to one-half of Athens' population beginning in 429 BCE. Kreon, Antigone's antagonist, displays the imperviousness to rational advice and lack of foresight exhibited by the politicians of Sophocles' era, whose follies Thucydides narrates, and which Sophocles himself was called in to help repair—specifically by taking a democracy that in a fit of imperial overreach suffered, in 413, a catastrophic defeat on the shores of Sicily, and replacing it with a revanchist oligarchy. When Pisander, one of the newly empowered oligarchs, asked Sophocles if he was one of the councilors who had approved the replacement of the democratic assembly by what was, in effect, a junta of four hundred, Sophocles admitted that he had. "Why?" asked Pisander. "Did you not think this a terrible decision?" Sophocles agreed it was. "So weren't you doing something terrible?" "That's right. There was no better alternative." (Aristotle, Rh. 1419a). The lesson? When life, more brutally than drama, delivers its irreversible calamities and judgments, it forces a polity, most movingly, to an utterly unanticipated, wholly 'other' moral and spiritual level.

In *Oedipus at Kolonos* Sophocles alludes to his city's decline when he celebrates a self-confident Athens that no longer existed when Sophocles wrote that play. He gives us Theseus, a throwback to the type of thoughtful, decisive, all-around leader Athens lacked as it pursued policies that left it impoverished and defenseless—this under the delusion that its only enemies were Spartans and Sparta's allies.

IV

Archaeologists have identified scores of local theaters all over the Greek world—stone semicircles, some in cities and at religious destinations, others in rural villages. Within many of these structures both ancient and modern plays are still staged. Hillsides whose slopes were wide and gentle enough to seat a crowd made perfect settings for dramatic encounters and were the earliest theaters. Ancient roads that widened below a gentle hillside, or level ground at a hill's base, provided suitable performance spaces. Such sites, along with every city's agora and a temple dedicated to Dionysos or another god, were the main arenas of community activity. Stone tablets along roads leading to theaters commemorated local victors: athletes, actors, playwrights, singers, and the winning plays' producers. Theaters, in every sense, were open to all the crosscurrents of civic and domestic life.

The components of the earliest theaters reflect their rural origins and were later incorporated into urban settings. *Theatron*, the root of our word "theater," translates as "viewing place" and designated the curved and banked seating area. *Orchestra* was literally "the place for dancing." The costumed actors emerged from and retired to the *skenê*, a word that originally meant, and literally was in the rural theaters, a tent. As theaters evolved to become more permanent structures, the *skenê* developed as well into a "stage building" whose painted facade changed, like a mask, with the characters' various habitats. Depending on the drama, the *skenê* could assume the appearance of a king's grand palace, the Kyklops' cave, a temple to a god, or (reverting to its original material form) an army commander's tent.

Greek drama itself originated in two earlier traditions, one rural, one civic. Choral singing of hymns to honor Dionysos or other gods and heroes, which had begun in the countryside, evolved into the structured choral ode. The costumes and the dancing of choral singers, often accompanied by a reed instrument, are depicted on sixth-century vases that predate the plays staged in the Athenian theater. The highly confrontational nature of every play suggests how early choral odes and dialogues came into being in concert with a fundamental aspect of democratic governance: public and spirited debate. Two or more characters facing off in front of an audience was a situation at the heart of both drama and democratic politics.

Debate, the democratic Athenian art practiced and perfected by politicians, litigators, and thespians—relished and judged by voters, juries, and audiences—flourished in theatrical venues and permeated daily Athenian life. Thucydides used it to narrate his history of the war between Athens and Sparta. He recalled scores of lengthy debates that laid out the motives of politicians, generals, and diplomats as each argued his case for a particular policy or a strategy. Plato, recognizing the open-ended, exploratory power of spirited dialogue, wrote his philosophy entirely in dramatic form.

The Greeks were addicted to contests and turned virtually every chance for determining a winner into a formal competition. The Great Dionysia for playwrights and choral singers and the Olympics for athletes are only the most famous and familiar. The verbal *agon* remains to this day a powerful medium for testing and judging issues. And character, as in the debate between Teukros and Menelaos, may be laid bare. But there is no guarantee. Persuasiveness can be, and frequently is, manipulative (e.g., many of the sophists evolved into hired rhetorical guns, as distinguished from the truth-seeking, pre-Socratic philosophers). Sophocles may well have had the sophists' amorality in mind when he had Odysseus persuade Neoptomolos that betraying Philoktetes would be a patriotic act and bring the young man fame.

Though they were part of a high-stakes competition, the plays performed at the Dionysia were part of a religious ceremony whose chief purpose was to honor theater's patron god, Dionysos. The god's worshippers believed that Dionysos' powers and rituals transformed the ways in which they experienced and dealt with their world—from their enthralled response to theatrical illusion and disguise to the exhilaration, liberation, and violence induced by wine. Yet the festival also aired, or licensed, civic issues that might otherwise have had no truly public, *polis*-wide expression. The playwrights wrote as *politai*, civic poets, as distinguished from those who focused on personal lyrics and shorter choral works. Though *Aias* and *Philoktetes* are set in a military milieu, the issues they engage are essentially civil and political. Neither *Aias* nor *Philoktetes* is concerned with the 'enemy of record,' Troy, but rather with Greek-on-Greek conflict. With civil disruption, and worse. In fact one need look no further than the play venue itself for confirmation of the interpenetration of the civic with the military—a concern bordering on preoccupation—when, every year, the orphans of warriors killed in battle were given new hoplite armor and a place of honor at the Festival of Dionysos.

Communal cohesiveness and the historical continuity of the polity are most tellingly threatened from within: in *Aias* by the individualistic imbalance and arrogance of Aias, whose warrior qualities and strengths are also his weakness—they lead him to destroy the war spoil that is the common property of the entire Greek army—and in *Philoktetes* by the understandable and just, yet inordinately unyielding, self-preoccupation of Philoktetes himself. In both cases the fundamental, encompassing question is this: With what understandings, what basic values, is the commonality of the *polis* to be recovered and rededicated in an era in which civic cohesiveness is under the extreme pressure of a war Athens is losing (especially at the time *Philoktetes* was produced) and, further, the simmering stasis of unresolved class or caste interests? In sharply different ways, all three plays of the Oedipus cycle, as well as *Aias* and *Elektra*, cast doubt on the legitimacy of usurped, authoritarian, or publicly disapproved leadership.

Given the historical and political dynamism of these great, instructive works, we've aimed to translate and communicate their challenge to Athenian values for a contemporary audience whose own values are no less under duress.

V

The Great Dionysia was the central and most widely attended event of the political year, scheduled after winter storms had abated so that foreign visitors could come and bear witness to Athens' wealth, civic pride, imperial power, and artistic imagination. For eight or nine days each spring, during the heyday of Greek theater in the fifth century BCE, Athenians flocked to the temple grounds sacred to Dionysos on the southern slope of the Acropolis. After dark on the first day, a parade of young men hefted a giant phallic icon of the god from the temple and into the nearby theater. As the icon had been festooned with garlands of ivy and a mask of the god's leering face, their raucous procession initiated a dramatic festival called the City Dionysia, a name that differentiated it from the festival's ancient rural origins in Dionysian myth and cult celebrations of the god. As the festival gained importance in the sixth century BCE, most likely through the policies of Pisistratus, it was also known as the Great Dionysia.

Pisistratus, an Athenian tyrant in power off and on beginning in 561 BCE and continuously from 546 to 527, had good reason for adapting the Rural Dionysia as Athens' Great Dionysia: "Dionysos was a god for the 'whole' of democratic Athens" (Hughes, 213). Everyone, regardless of political faction or social standing, could relate to the boisterous communal activities of the festival honoring Dionysos: feasting, wine drinking, dancing, singing, romping through the countryside, and performing or witnessing dithyrambs and more elaborate dramatic works. The Great Dionysia thus served to keep in check, if not transcend, internal factionalizing by giving all citizens a 'natural' stake in Athens—Athens not simply as a place but as a venerable polity with ancient cultural roots. To this end Pisistratus had imported from Eleutherai an ancient phallic representation of Dionysos, one that took several men to carry.

Lodged as it was in a temple on the outskirts of Athens, this bigger-than-life icon gave the relatively new, citified cult the sanctified air of hoary antiquity (Csapo and Slater, 103–104). Thus validated culturally, the Great Dionysia was secured as a host to reassert, and annually rededicate, Athens as a democratic polity. As Bettany Hughes notes in *The Hemlock Cup*, "to call Greek drama an 'art-form' is somewhat anachronistic. The Greeks (unlike many modern-day bureaucrats) didn't distinguish drama as 'art'—something separate from 'society,' 'politics,' [or] 'life.' Theater was fundamental to democratic Athenian business. . . . [In] the fifth century this was the place where Athenian democrats came to understand the very world they lived in" (Hughes, 213).

The occasion offered Athens the chance to display treasure exacted from subjugated 'allies' (or tributes others willingly brought to the stage) and to award gold crowns to citizens whose achievements Athens' leaders wished to honor. Theater attendance itself was closely linked to citizenship; local town councils issued free festival passes to citizens in good standing. The ten generals elected yearly to conduct Athens' military campaigns poured libations to Dionysos. The theater's bowl seethed with a heady, sometimes unruly brew of military, political, and religious energy.

Performances began at dawn and lasted well into the

afternoon. The 14,000 or more Athenians present watched in god knows what state of anticipation or anxiety. Whatever else it did to entertain, move, and awe, Athenian tragedy consistently exposed human vulnerability to the gods' malice and favoritism. Because the gods were potent realities to Athenian audiences, they craved and expected an overwhelming emotional, physically distressing experience. That expectation distinguishes the greater intensity with which Athenians responded to plays from our own less challenging, more routine and frequent encounters with drama. Athenians wept while watching deities punish the innocent or unlucky, a reaction that distressed Plato. In his *Republic*, rather than question the motives or morality of the all-powerful Olympian gods for causing mortals grief, he blamed the poets and playwrights for their unwarranted wringing of the audience's emotions. He held that the gods had no responsibility for human suffering. True to form, Plato banned both poets and playwrights from his ideal city.

Modern audiences would be thoroughly at home with other, more cinematic stage effects. The sights and sounds tragedy delivered in the Theater of Dionysos were often spectacular. Aristotle, who witnessed a lifetime of productions in the fourth century—well after Sophocles' own lifetime, when the plays were performed in the heat of their historical moment—identified "spectacle," or *opsis*, as one of the basic (though to him suspect) elements of tragic theater. Under the influence of Aristotle, who preferred the study to the stage, and who therefore emphasized the poetry rather than the production of works, ancient commentators tended to consider "the visual aspects of drama [as] both vulgar and archaic" (Csapo and Slater, 257).

Nonetheless, visual and aural aspects there were: oboe music; dancing and the singing of set-piece odes by a chorus; masks that transformed the same male actor, for instance, into a swarthy-faced young hero, a dignified matron, Argos with a hundred eyes, or the Kyklops with only one. The theater featured painted scenery and large-scale constructions engineered with sliding platforms and towering cranes. It's hardly surprising that Greek tragedy has been considered a forerunner of Italian opera.

Judges awarding prizes at the Great Dionysia were chosen by lot from a list supplied by the council—one judge from each of Athens' ten tribes. Critical acumen was not required to get one's name on the list, but the *choregoi* (the producers and financial sponsors of the plays) were present when the jury was assembled and probably had a hand in its selection. At the conclusion of the festival the ten selected judges, each having sworn that he hadn't been bribed or unduly influenced, would inscribe on a tablet the names of the three competing playwrights in descending order of merit. The rest of the process depended on chance. The ten judges placed their ballots in a large urn. The presiding official drew five at random, counted up the weighted vote totals, and declared the winner.

VI

When Sophocles was a boy, masters trained him to excel in music, dance, and wrestling. He won crowns competing against his age-mates in all three disciplines. Tradition has it that he first appeared in Athenian national life at age fifteen, dancing naked (according to one source) and leading other boy dancers in a hymn of gratitude to celebrate Athens' defeat of the Persian fleet in the straits of Salamis.

Sophocles' father, Sophroniscus, manufactured weapons and armor (probably in a factory operated by slaves), and his mother, Phaenarete, was a midwife. The family lived in Kolonos, a rural suburb just north of Athens. Although his parents were not aristocrats, as most other playwrights' were, they surely had money and owned property; thus their status did not hamper their son's career prospects. Sophocles' talents as a dramatist, so formidable and so precociously developed, won him early fame. As an actor he triumphed in his own now-lost play, *Nausicaä*, in the role of the eponymous young princess who discovers the nearly naked Odysseus washed up on the beach while playing ball with her girlfriends.

During Sophocles' sixty-five-year career as a *didaskalos* he wrote and directed more than 120 plays and was awarded first prize at least eighteen times. No record exists of his placing lower than second. Of the seven entire works of his that survive, along with a substantial fragment of a satyr play, *The Trackers*, only two very late plays can be given exact production dates: *Philoktetes* in 409 and *Oedipus at Kolonos,* staged posthumously in 401. Some evidence suggests that *Antigone* was produced around 442–441 and *Oedipus the King* in the 420s. *Aias*, *Elektra*, and *Women of Trakhis* have been conjecturally, but never conclusively, dated through stylistic analysis. Aristotle, who had access we forever lack to the hundreds of fifth-century plays produced at the Dionysia, preferred Sophocles to his rivals Aeschylus and Euripides. He considered *Oedipus the King* the perfect example of tragic form, and developed his theory of tragedy from his analysis of it.

Sophocles' fellow citizens respected him sufficiently to vote him into high city office on at least three occasions. He served for a year as chief tribute-collector for Athens' overseas empire. A controversial claim by Aristophanes of Byzantium, in the third century, implies that Sophocles' tribe was so impressed by a production of *Antigone* that they voted him in as one of ten military generals (*strategoi*) in 441–440. Later in life Sophocles was respected as a participant in democratic governance at the highest level. In 411 he was elected to a ten-man commission charged with replacing Athens' discredited democratic governance with an oligarchy, a development that followed the military's catastrophic defeat in Sicily in 413.

Most ancient biographical sources attest to Sophocles' good looks, his easygoing manner, and his enjoyment of life. Athanaeus' multivolume *Deipnosophistai*, a compendium of gossip and dinner chat about and among ancient worthies, includes several vivid passages that reveal Sophocles as both a commanding presence and an impish prankster, ready one moment to put down a schoolmaster's boorish literary criticism and the next to flirt with the wine boy.

Sophocles is also convincingly described as universally respected, with amorous inclinations and intensely religious qualities that, to his contemporaries, did not seem incompatible. Religious piety meant something quite different to an Athenian than the humility, sobriety, and aversion to sensual pleasure it might suggest to us—officially, if not actually. His involvement in various cults, including one dedicated to a god of health and another to the hero Herakles, contributed to his reputation as "loved by the gods" and "the most religious of men." He was celebrated—and worshipped after his death as a hero—for bringing a healing cult (related to Aesculapius and involving a snake) to Athens. It is possible he founded an early version of a hospital. He never flinched from portraying the Greek gods as often wantonly cruel, destroying innocent people, for instance, as punishment for their ancestors' crimes. But the gods in *Antigone*, *Oedipus at Kolonos*, and *Philoktetes* mete out justice with a more even hand.

One remarkable absence in Sophocles' own life was documented suffering of any kind. His luck continued to the moment his body was placed in its tomb. As he lay dying, a Spartan army had once again invaded the Athenian countryside, blocking access to Sophocles' burial site beyond Athens' walls. But after Sophocles' peaceful death the Spartan general allowed the poet's burial party to pass through his lines, apparently out of respect for the god Dionysos.

Robert Bagg

James Scully

NOTE

1. Unless otherwise indicated, the line numbers and note numbers for translations of Sophocles' dramas other than *Philoktetes* refer to those in the Harper Perennial *Complete Sophocles* series.

INTRODUCTION
SOPHOCLES AT 87

Philoktetes. First performed in 409 BCE,
when Sophocles was 87 years old.

Philoktetes—with a festering, god-given wound in his
foot—has been abandoned on the desolate island of
Lemnos by the Greeks under Odysseus. They couldn't
stand the stench, nor his screams of pain. That was ten years
ago. Since then, they've learned they can't take Troy without
Philoktetes and the bow given to him by Herakles—nor without
Neoptolemos, son of the dead Achilles. Yet Philoktetes would
rather kill Odysseus than return to Troy. It's up to Neoptolemos, inveigled by Odysseus, to trick Philoktetes into returning.
Odysseus, an opportunistic character representing the Greek
army, will use any means to carry out his mission. Philoktetes
and Neoptolemos, however, are constantly at sea: shifting and
re-shifting amidst mixed feelings, deceptions, suspicions, and
qualms as they struggle with themselves and their obscurely
evolving relationship.

There are many plays within this play. Philoktetes and Neoptolemos are driven not only by unbidden psychologies but by
their through lines: the specific ends they want to achieve. With

the scenario given him by Odysseus, Neoptolemos is caught between playing a character, a curtailed version of himself, and being his own person. He has a tenuous grip on his role. That, plus pressure from the nakedly visceral Philoktetes—by turns friendly, even fatherly, and bitterly hostile—will wear him down. Remarkably, there are no offstage events in this pressure cooker of a play. Everything happens in the moment, up close and personal. (The false Merchant and his tale are themselves an event, not the report of one.) Once Odysseus's hooks are set—in Neoptolemos and, through him, in Philoktetes—there's no let up.

Philoktetes is a discarded veteran of the Trojan War. He is as well a generic old man—sick, smelly, cantankerous, a burden abandoned in a seemingly blank space. Yet he isn't expendable. The Greeks can't win the war without him. Further, it seems elders in general are socially necessary. Curious about former comrades, Philoktetes asks if the "old and honest" Nestor is still alive—adding, with the hated sons of Atreus in mind: "He's the one / could baffle their schemes with wise advice" (471–472). He wonders what future may be envisioned without the 'good' people—the likes of Nestor, or the dead Achilles and Aias. "What's to be our outlook on life / when *they're* dead, and Odysseus, / who *should* be dead, isn't!" (478–480).

The novice Neoptolemos and the old hand, Philoktetes, occupy the opposite poles of a historical-*cum*-cultural continuum that is rediscovering itself over a dead space: the 'deadness' is not Lemnos, however, but the cynical, soulless present of Odysseus.[1] Objectively, Odysseus does have the right end in view. The goal to unite Neoptolemos, Philoketes, and Herakles' bow to capture Troy and so end the war is beyond question in this play. But Odysseus's crudely instrumentalist *means* lack the cultural and historical integrity, the broth of trust, needed to achieve that end.

Philoktetes' affliction is intolerable. His intransigence, exasperating. He wants to be cured but refuses to be cured—wants to leave Lemnos but refuses to leave—*if* that means returning to the Greek camp at Troy. On the face of it, his stubbornness doesn't make sense. Yet sense is also made extratextually. Brecht noted that production, unlike scripting, is risky. No one can predict how the 'acting out' will turn out. There are tones of voice, timings, silences. And bodies. Here there's extraordinary emphasis on the raw physicality of Philoktetes: from the crudity of his utensils to the stench haunting his every appeal for passage home to Oita. His eyeballs roll up into his head. His frequent outbursts, his screams, are not notational or formulaic but spontaneous and unbridled. Or, worse, gagged on themselves. These too make sense, but transmitted somatically rather than conceptually. It comes in shock waves of extratextual information. As these weigh in, his obstinacy, the most 'senseless' thing about him, accumulates yet another kind of sense. But to get it we need the kinesthetic, blow-by-blow feel of *being* Philoktetes, whose deepest wound is not in his body but in his spirit. What rationality or sensibleness is sufficient to cure that?

Given his awful solitude, not hearing another human voice, Philoktetes has vested the island, parts of his own body, and aspects of his affliction with vital existences of their own: his suppurating foot, his eyes, the intermittent fever: "this

wandering disease [that] comes to me / when it's tired wandering, / and having had enough / it goes away" (832–836). Birds,
cliffs, cave, breaking waves, nymphs of marshy meadows—all
these and more he grants the feeling life *of*. That is, he accepts
that they have their own conscious existence, independent of
him. This is sometimes taken as personification, yet is the an-
tithesis of that. It stems not from anthropomorphism but something akin to animism—a relation to the natural world that
respects the self-driven integrity of that world. Here it also testifies to the uncanny power emanating from the root *being* of this
ancient world and its Dionysian drama. Grasping that, we may
appreciate the generative power Philoktetes draws from a natural world that would otherwise, without the fuming *gravitas* of
his passion, lapse into the unredeemed desolation of Lemnos.
His immense will to live has vitalized what others, who have not
lived his life, see only as a dead land. Now, having made a life
on Lemnos—however poor and hard that life is—Philoktetes'
decision not to go back to Troy makes a counterintuitive, but
not incomprehensible, sense.[2]

Nevertheless, socially, and therefore humanly, his decision
not to return to Troy is the wrong one. Self-preoccupied after
so many years struggling to stay alive, utterly alone, he cannot come to the right, civically called-for decision: to rescue
the Greek forces that betrayed and abandoned him. It takes
Herakles to socialize (in the technical sense of 'civilize' or de-
individualize) the grounds Philoktetes stands on—and to give
those grounds staying power by historicizing them. Herakles'
bow testifies to their mutual history. It was Philoktetes who lit
the funeral pyre when Herakles, writhing in agony from the

poisoned shirt given him by Deianeira, could find no one else willing to do it. If Herakles is a deus ex machina he is, as well, an all-too-human hero out of Philoktetes' past, when Herakles himself was desperate for help, and Philoktetes gave it.

Philoktetes was performed four years after the defeat of the Greek fleet at Syracuse, and two years after the first oligarchic coup in 411 BCE. Democracy was restored the following year, but the ongoing *stasis* (i.e., a 'standing' apart or against, a state of civil strife) portended the end of the Athenian empire. This was five years before the absolute end, when the walls of Athens were razed and an oligarchic constitution was installed under the *dunasteia*—the 'collective tyranny' or junta—of the Thirty Tyrants in 404–403 BCE. Given the protracted turmoil of the times, it would seem Herakles speaks as much to the Athenian audience as to Philoktetes. Reaching deeper than the factionalism that was surely rife in Athens, Herakles delivers the final word on what is right, what is holy, what Zeus ordains. He tells Philoktetes what is required of him, predicting his cure and his success at Troy. Yet 'success' isn't everything. Just as significantly, Herakles goes on to demonstrate the proper attitude Philoktetes must have in victory: "You will sack Troy and be honored / with the choicest spoils. Bring these / home with you to the Oitan highlands / to please your father, Poias. The other / spoils such as common soldiers get / lay on my funeral pyre: as a tribute / to my bow" (1615–1621). Herakles, the most illustrious of warriors, lines himself up with ordinary soldiers, setting aside his own aristocratic, heroic prerogative. How could Philoktetes do less?

What then of Neoptolemos, whom we witness coming of

age—an ambitious, righteous, initially callow youth mellowed by Philoktetes and growing into a morally conscient, yet no less ambitious, maturity? Herakles has words for him as well. He doesn't name Neoptolemos—technically, he's still addressing Philoktetes—but the Greek audience would have known to whom the words referred: "Yet remember, when / you sack Troy show piety toward all things / relating to the gods. To Zeus, nothing / matters more. The sacred doesn't die / when men do. Whether they live or die, / holiness endures" (1631–36). Some values are sacralized: they transcend the moment, outlasting factions and parties. Yet even as Herakles makes this pronouncement, the audience knows that the youth we've watched growing fitfully into a decent, feeling man will become notorious for his savagery at the conquest of Troy—among other atrocities, killing old Priam, whom his own father Achilles had spared, at the altar of Zeus. Is nothing, then, to be sacred? Sophocles' vision toward the end of his long life, very nearly at the end of the Athenian empire, is not for the faint of heart.

NOTES

1. A view close to that of Sophocles—because its baseline is not one stratum of a stratified polity, but the whole of the polity, however internally stratified that whole may be—is articulated by Enzo Siciliano in remarks on the poet Pier Paolo Pasolini: "The [young] Pasolini already had clearly in mind the idea that *it is lethal in a collectivity to break, cast aside or forget historical continuity to the point of denying it—and history is a synthesis of languages, customs and usages. The ideal of action, in such a poet, was directed, then, toward the*

defense of that 'continuity,' that 'historicity.' " In *Aias* as well as in *Philoktetes,* Sophocles assumes a comparably deep commitment to 'historicity.'

Given how "fragile and fractious" Athens became, especially from 461 BCE on, though plays "might be matchless in their honesty, with their forensic analysis of the extremes of the human condition, their investigation of human flaws . . . [they were also] where you came to process information, to learn to form an opinion of the world around you, and love your *polis*. . . . The experience of theater was meant to be one that reaffirmed Athens' [once] robust sense of *dêmos*-solidarity" (Hughes, 214–215, 262).

2. Philoktetes' refusal of salvation evokes depictions of a miserably risen Lazarus, or Donatello's rendering of Christ's Resurrection (in San Lorenzo, Florence). The comparison is not of individuals, certainly, but of their outlooks. The Resurrection is by definition a glorious event, yet Donatello shows the risen Christ drastically aged and stooped, clinging to his staff at the edge of his tomb as—melancholy beyond belief—he looks out onto the world: he had to come back to *this*? Not a rational response to his salvation, yet it does make sense. As does Philoktetes' tenacious refusal of an offer that, on the face of it, he should not be able to refuse. When Philoktetes does come round he does so spontaneously—not in the name of success, nor of a cure (he reasons nothing out), but responding instinctively to a vision and a 'call' of such scale and cultural depth it is irresistible.

Philoktetes

Cliff on the desolate island of Lemnos. Ocean below. Occasional glowing
above Mosychlos, a distant volcano. ODYSSEUS appears, followed by
NEOPTOLEMOS and one of his sailors (unseen). Sounds of the sea.

ODYSSEUS

     This is it!
Lemnos. A no-man's-land
in nowhere but ocean. No one
comes here, no one lives here.
Now, Neoptolemos, as you're truly the son
of Achilles, the noblest of all the Greeks,
listen to me.

        It's here years ago
I put Philoktetes the Malian, son of Poias,
ashore . . . *under orders from the chiefs*   10
of course . . . what with his foot all
runny with pus from a flesh-eating sore,
well, we couldn't get a moment's peace!
couldn't start the sacrifice, never mind
the wine offering, what with his
screaming, hollering, it was a bad sign,
it never let up! But that's . . . too much
to get into. This is no time for talk.
If he catches me here my scheme
to take him is wasted. From now on   20
it's your job to help me carry this out.
Look for a rock cave like a tunnel.
In cold weather, early or late in the day,
there's always a sunny spot to sit in.
In summer a cool breeze blows through
bringing sleep. Below, to the left,
there should be a bubbling spring
to drink from—if it's not dried up.

Easy now. Go see. Signal me if he's
still there, or should we look elsewhere,   30
then we'll know what to do. I'll tell you,
you'll listen. Together we can pull this off.

NEOPTOLEMOS **cranes to look.**

NEOPTOLEMOS

Odysseus, sir, what you're looking for is here.
That cave? I think I see it.

ODYSSEUS

Above you? Below? I can't see from here.

NEOPTOLEMOS

Above. No footsteps, far as I can hear.

ODYSSEUS

Watch out he's not sleeping in there.

NEOPTOLEMOS

Now I see. Empty, yes, nobody's there.

ODYSSEUS

No sign anyone lives there?

NEOPTOLEMOS

Yes. A bed of leaves pressed down   40
like it's been slept on.

ODYSSEUS

Nothing else in there? That's it?

NEOPTOLEMOS looks into the cave.

NEOPTOLEMOS

A wooden cup. Rough, poorly made.
And some kindling.

ODYSSEUS

Those would be his all right.

NEOPTOLEMOS

And rags drying in the sun. *Whew!*
Loaded with pus.

ODYSSEUS

That clinches it. He lives here. Can't be far off.
How far could he get with a rotting foot? No,
he's out scrounging for food, or some herb   50
to ease the pain. . . . Send your man to watch out
so he doesn't catch me off guard. Of all the Greeks
I'm the one he *really* wants to get his hands on.

NEOPTOLEMOS

(gestures off)
Say no more. He's going. Consider it done.

Sailor (unseen) leaves, as NEOPTOLEMOS stares after him.

He'll look out. But you were saying . . . ?

ODYSSEUS

As the son of Achilles you must carry out
your mission. But you can't just put

your *body* into it.
You may hear something *mmm* 'novel.'
Some plan you haven't heard yet. Well   60
you have to go along with it. That's what
you're here for.

NEOPTOLEMOS

What are your orders?

ODYSSEUS

As you're giving him your story
reach into his soul. Take it! He asks
who you are, where you're from, tell him
straight out: you're the son of Achilles.
Can't lie about that. Only you're headed home,
you've left the Greek fleet, you hate them. After
they'd begged you, prayed you, to leave your home   70
hey, you were their only hope of taking Troy
they didn't think you deserved Achilles' armor
or arms! wouldn't give them to you when you
claimed them; by rights they were yours! Instead
they handed them over to *Odysseus*. Say
anything you want about me, nothing's too nasty,
I couldn't care less—but if you don't do this
the whole Greek army will be demoralized. Just
get that bow. If you don't, you'll never take Troy.

It's you who will have to deal with him.   80
He'll trust you. Me, never. *You* didn't
come to Troy bound by an oath. You came

on your own, not forced to—unlike those
of us who came on that first expedition.
He sees me, and has that bow, I'm dead,
and you are too, my comrade in doom.
No, here's how we have to approach this:
as the bow is unbeatable, you have to be
clever enough to steal it.

        O . . . I know, it's not like you   90
my boy, to say or do anything out of line.
Yet to succeed is such a sweet thing,
go for it! We can be honest some other time.
Give yourself to me but one short, shameless
               stretch of day.
Then, forever after, you're free to be known
as the very soul of honor.

NEOPTOLEMOS

Son of Laertes, advice I can't stand to hear
I'd hate to act on. It's not in me
to scheme and lie. It wasn't in my father,   100
either. Everyone says so. I'd sooner
take him head on, not sneak around. He's got
one good foot! Can't get the best of us on *that*.
Of course I'm here to help you, do as you say.
I'd hate to be called a traitor. Yet I'd rather do
what's right, and fail, than succeed by deceit.

ODYSSEUS

You *are* your father's son. Brave man.
At your age, just like you, my hand

was quicker than my tongue.
But now I've learned it's words   110
that move people, not deeds.

NEOPTOLEMOS
Then you're ordering me to lie?

ODYSSEUS
I'm telling you: *disarm* Philoktetes.

NEOPTOLEMOS
By being 'disarming'? Why not
persuade him straight out?

ODYSSEUS
He won't listen. And then force *won't* work.

NEOPTOLEMOS
What is it makes him so sure of himself?

ODYSSEUS
Arrows definite as the death they deliver.

NEOPTOLEMOS
No one dares approach him then!

ODYSSEUS
No. Unless . . . you insinuate yourself.   120

NEOPTOLEMOS

You don't think it's shameful? To tell lies?

ODYSSEUS

Not if lying gets us through this
dragged-out war.

NEOPTOLEMOS

Won't the look on my face give me away?

ODYSSEUS

Look to what's in it for you! Can't be shy about it.

NEOPTOLEMOS

What good's it do *me* if he comes to Troy?

ODYSSEUS

Troy is taken . . . only with his arrows.

NEOPTOLEMOS

I'm not going to take Troy? Like you said?

ODYSSEUS

Not you without them. Nor them without you.

NEOPTOLEMOS

Well, if that's how it is, we'll have to go get them.   130

ODYSSEUS

You do that, you're coming away with *two* prizes.

NEOPTOLEMOS

Two? Tell me, and I won't hesitate.

ODYSSEUS

You'll be called both shrewd *and* brave.

NEOPTOLEMOS

Then no matter what, I'll do it. No shame.

ODYSSEUS

Remember what I told you then? Understood?

NEOPTOLEMOS

(irritated)

Yes! I'll do it. Now that I've said I would.

ODYSSEUS

Wait here. He'll show up. I'm leaving
so he doesn't see me here, with you.
I'll take the lookout back to your ship.
If you're running late I'll send him back   140
dressed like the skipper of a merchant ship.
The disguise will help. He'll spin a yarn,
you pay attention! he's feeding you leads,
go along with him. I'm going to the ship
now. But you know what you have to do.

May Hermes, who knows the way, lead us
on, and Victory, along with Athena
        Defender of Athens
who always watches over me!

*ODYSSEUS slips away. CHORUS of NEOPTOLEMOS's sailors (mostly
older than he) approach from the shore below. They cannot see
the cave.*

CHORUS
(severally)
        Sir: 150
what should we say, what
        not say?
we're strangers in a strange land,
this hermit will be suspicious!
Instruct us.

The cleverest
        of the clever,
the wisest advice, comes from
the one Zeus gave his godly scepter to.
        You, still in youth,   160
have had this passed down to you.

So tell us, how can we serve you?

NEOPTOLEMOS
For now, you might look at the sea-cliff cave
        he holes up in.

Don't worry, it's OK. But when this
dread figure works his way back
          be ready.
If I signal you, come running. Help
as best you can.

LEADER

We've been watching out for you   170
a long time now, sir. But at least
tell how he shelters himself. Where?
We need to know he can't sneak up on us.
Where does his foot touch the ground
          now? In there
or out here somewhere?

NEOPTOLEMOS

Well, you see where he lives up here.
Two openings. Rock . . .

LEADER

But the cursèd creature! *Where* is *he*?

NEOPTOLEMOS

I'm sure he's dragging his agony around   180
hereabouts, looking for food. Word is
that's how he lives: looking for game
          to kill
with his wingèd arrows.
Rotten miserable as he is,
no one comes to him with a cure.

CHORUS
(severally)

I feel sorry for him: a man

no one cares for

with the face of a man

no one lives with,   190

alone always in pain.

Each time he feels a new need

bewildering him, his mind wanders.

How does he go on?

Dark are the doings of the gods. Unlucky

the strains of men

whose resources fall short of their doom.

This man's as wellborn

as anyone. Yet here

stripped of all life gives,   200

even human company,

he lies alone

among dappled or shaggy beasts—

pitiful, tormented, hungering,

his pain incurable

the while the garbling Echo looms

from afar

crying back at him his own crying.

NEOPTOLEMOS

There's no mystery in it. From the beginning

the gods, I believe, were in on this,   210

working through the vicious Chrysē.
All his suffering all alone
        comes from a god—
to keep him from bending his almighty bow
        against Troy—
until the time comes
when the city *must* fall.

LEADER
Shsh!

NEOPTOLEMOS
What now?

CHORUS
(severally)
A sound came up!   220
Like what a man would make
excruciated by pain!

Over there!
        Or there! Listen,
listen! Such pain
                dragging this way!

The voice of a man, sure now, sounding
the anguish of his way.

LEADER
Time now sir . . .

NEOPTOLEMOS

      Why, what . . . ?   230

LEADER

Change of plans!

        He's almost here!

That's no shepherd piping his way

home from pasture, no

    it's *him*

stumbling, his moan carrying

a long way in pain seeing

nothing moored in the sea out there.

PHILOKTETES—in rags, foot wrapped in filthy bandages, bow in hand—is on them . . .

PHILOKTETES

        Strangers!

Who? From where? What brings you   240

rowing ashore

to this desolate island? And no harbor!?

What is your country? Who are your people?

Dressed like Greeks. I like that

        more than anything.

Speak! It's OK, don't let the wild look of me

scare you off. Don't panic. Have pity

    on a lonely miserable man,

say something if you really come as friends—

just answer!   250

It wouldn't be right,
us not exchanging words with one another.

NEOPTOLEMOS

Since you ask, sir, the first thing
you should know is: we're Greeks.

PHILOKTETES

O music to the ears! After so long
to hear Greek from such as you!
         Dear boy
what brought you to this place?
This very spot! What necessity? What urge?
         What most   260
merciful wind pushed you this way?
Tell me everything so I can know
who you are.

NEOPTOLEMOS

I'm sailing home to the island of Skyros.
I am Neoptolemos, son of Achilles.
Now you know everything.

PHILOKTETES

O my son of a beloved father,
         a beloved land,
brought up by your grandfather Lykomedes—
what's your mission here? Where are you coming from?   270

NEOPTOLEMOS

Right now I'm sailing from Troy.

PHILOKTETES

O? How so? For sure *you* weren't with us
when we first set sail for Troy.

NEOPTOLEMOS

You!? Were actually part of *that*!

PHILOKTETES

My boy, I'm standing here. You don't know me!?

NEOPTOLEMOS

Know you? How? I've never seen you before.

PHILOKTETES

Never heard my name? No word
of the miseries killing me to death?

NEOPTOLEMOS

Nothing. I don't know what you're talking about.

PHILOKTETES

I'm lost! The gods hate me!   280
Not one word of me abandoned here
has reached my home. No word
to Greeks anywhere out there!
The men who brought me here

in silence, in secret, make
mockery of me
while my disease
flourishes its worst, and spreads.

O my boy . . . Achilles' son . . .
I'm one you *must* have heard of!   290
the master of Herakles' bow!
      Philoktetes, son of Poias!
whom those two commanders and Odysseus
tricked and dumped
in this emptiness to waste away
with this vicious sickness,
venom-stricken by a vicious serpent.

Sickness I was left alone with.

The fleet had put in here
      having left sea-locked Chrysē.   300
They'd set me ashore. From rocking
on the stormy waters I'd fallen exhausted,
     they were glad to see,
asleep under an arch of rock. They left
some rags good enough for a beggar
and a little food. Me too they left
and may the gods give them the same.

Can you feel, son, how *I* felt, waking
to nobody here?

I burst into tears.   310
Can you feel how I felt cursing myself
seeing the very ships I'd sailed on
        gone! and on the island
nobody, not one human being
to give me a hand when I went down
        in pain? All I *saw*
was pain. Plenty of it.

Time passed me by. Season after season
cramped alone in my cave, I made do
myself. Had to. For something to eat   320
this bow knocked down fluttering doves.
The bowstring, as I released it, hummed!
        . . . then
whatever I'd hit I had to go after,
step & drag,
hauling this goddam foot.
Had to get water too. And winters
with frost, the water frozen,
step & drag, get
firewood to cut up.   330
No fire, none, but striking
stone on stone
I'd make the secret spark
leap up, out of darkness!
And this is what saved me.
A roof overhead, fire,
it's all I need—except
release from this disease.

Young man, I'll tell you something
about this place. No sailor   340
drops by on purpose—there's no harbor,
no port to trade in, no 'entertainment.'
No man in his right mind comes here.
Well, suppose some do. A lot happens
in the course of a lifetime. Then,
my boy, they feel sorry for me,
or so they say. And give me food
and clothing. But what they won't do,
when I can bring myself to mention it,
is take me home.   350

Ten miserable years now
I'm rotting away, feeding
this disease
it can't get enough of me!
This the sons of Atreus and ruthless Odysseus
              did to me.
May the Gods of Above give them what I got.

LEADER

I too feel for you, son of Poias,
much as those others did.

NEOPTOLEMOS

And I can testify to the truth of what you say.   360
I know, having been overridden
by the sons of Atreus—and the brutish Odysseus.

PHILOKTETES

You too? Have a grudge against those damned
sons of Atreus? On what grounds?

NEOPTOLEMOS

O if only my anger might find its hands!
Mycenaeans and Spartans alike would know
Skyros, too, raises great warriors.

PHILOKTETES

You said it, boy! But what *is* it
you in your anger go after them for?

NEOPTOLEMOS

Sir, I will tell you—*gods* it's hard   370
to talk about! but when I got to Troy
they humiliated me. Because when
fate gripped Achilles, and made him die . . .

PHILOKTETES

Wait! Enough! Let me get this straight.
He's dead? *Achilles!?*

NEOPTOLEMOS

Dead. Killed not by a man but a god.
An arrow from Apollo.

PHILOKTETES

No! . . . Noble killer, noble killed.
Where now should I begin? Ask how
they wronged you? Or mourn the dead?   380

NEOPTOLEMOS

You have enough to do mourning yourself,
poor man. No need to mourn others.

PHILOKTETES

True enough. Well go on then. Tell me
exactly how they insulted you.

NEOPTOLEMOS

They came for me in a ship, the prow
all decked out, colors flying—
the great Odysseus, and Phoinix
who'd raised my father from infancy—
saying (true or not, I don't know)
since my father was dead, it was fated   390
no one could capture Troy *but me.*
That was their story.
                    It was all they needed to say.
I didn't wait to hear any more, but got myself
ready in a hurry. I wanted so to see my father
unburied. In all my life I'd never seen him
alive! Then too, they promised me that
when I got there, I alone could sack Troy.

Second day out, rowing along
          with a following wind   400
we landed at still painful Sigeion.

Soon as we hit shore, soldiers
crowded round, all swearing that
in me the dead Achilles lived again.
But he, he *was* dead. I wept for him, I felt
terrible. Then I went to the sons of Atreus,
figuring them as friends—to claim my father's arms
and whatever else he'd left. And, well . . .
they had the nerve to say: "Son of Achilles
take everything else of his, but those arms   410
belong to another man. The son of Laertes."

I choked up with rage and grief:
"You dared give away my arms
without so much as asking *me*?"

Then Odysseus—standing right there!—
he said: "That's right, boy. I saved them
and the remains of their owner."

I called him everything under the sun
          I was so mad I, I
didn'tleaveanythingout, no, what with   420
him thinking he could steal my arms!
And I *got* to him. He doesn't usually
get mad, but, you know, he did, he said:

"Your duty was here. But *you* weren't.
Now your mouth spits such insolence
you'll never take those arms back to Skyros."

Bawled out, disrespected, I sail home now—
robbed of what I had coming to me
by the sleaziest of a sleazy breed: Odysseus.
Even so, I don't blame him so much as the sons   430
of Atreus. An army, like a city, depends
completely on its leaders. When men trample on
others' rights, they get that from their leaders.
Anyway. That's my story. May the gods bless
any enemy of the sons of Atreus. *I* do.

CHORUS

Goddess of Mountains,
Bountiful Earth,
Mother of Zeus himself,
you through whom flows
Paktolos' great rush   440
of gold dust

Wondrous Mother
there too I called on you
that day the sons of Atreus
puffed up with arrogance
piled insults on this man,
giving his father's revered armor
to that son of Laertes

I prayed you then—now

hear me   450

Dread Mother who rides

lions that slaughter bulls

PHILOKTETES

Friends, the grief you've brought with you

rings true.

Your story tells my story. In it I see

the machinations of the sons of Atreus

and Odysseus. That one will talk up

any shady agenda—do *anything* for

any unconscionable end. Nothing new

in that. What's strange is how Aias   460

if he was there, could put up with this.

NEOPTOLEMOS

My friend . . . he wasn't! If he had been alive

they would never have robbed me like that.

PHILOKTETES

Him too!? Dead?

NEOPTOLEMOS

Think of him as gone . . . out, from the world of light.

PHILOKTETES

It can't be! And yet Diomedes and Odysseus,

the bastard Sisyphos begot then sold to Laertes—

the ones who should be dead—aren't!?

NEOPTOLEMOS

Those ones? Believe it, right now they're riding
high in the Greek army.   470

PHILOKTETES

What of my friend, the old and honest Nestor of Pylos?
        Alive still? He's the one
could baffle their schemes with wise advice.

NEOPTOLEMOS

It's no longer in him. He lost his son
Antilochos, who cared for him.

PHILOKTETES

Damn! Those two you mention, they're
the last ones I want to hear are dead.
What's to be our outlook on life
when *they're* dead, and Odysseus
who *should* be dead, isn't!   480

NEOPTOLEMOS

He's a cagey wrestler, Philoktetes, yet
even clever moves may be upended.

PHILOKTETES

Gods Above! where was Patroklos
        he didn't help you out?
He was your father's dearest friend.

NEOPTOLEMOS

Dead. Him too. The short of it
is: war doesn't single out evil men
but in general kills the good.

PHILOKTETES

I'll vouch for that. Speaking of which,
how goes the worthless one   490
with the quick, nasty tongue?

NEOPTOLEMOS

That would be Odysseus?

PHILOKTETES

Not *him*. Thersites, that one.
We had no way, ever, to shut him up
though everyone tried. He still alive?

NEOPTOLEMOS

I haven't seen him myself. I *heard* he is.

PHILOKTETES

He would be. Nothing evil ever dies.
The gods swaddle it up. They take
some kind of pleasure keeping
the slick smooth ones out of Hades,   500
yet send the just and the good away,
down there forever. What
can I make of this? How can I
go along with them when,

while praising all things divine,
I see the gods are evil?

NEOPTOLEMOS

As for me, O son of an Oitan father,
I'll be steering clear of Troy, keeping
my distance from the sons of Atreus.
Where the worst men overpower the best,   510
where the good die, while cowards rule,
I won't ever put up with such men.
From now on it's rockbound Skyros
for me. I will live my life
happily, at home . . .
(pause; then, abruptly . . .)
Well! Got to get back to the ship!
Good-bye son of Poias. Good luck
        with the gods!
Here's hoping they cure you
just as you wish!   520
(to sailors, all business)
Let's get going. We should be set to sail
the moment the heavens permit.

PHILOKTETES

          Already!? Going?

NEOPTOLEMOS

Yes. We need to be aboard
ready to sail when the wind shifts.

PHILOKTETES

My son, I beg you, in the name of
your father your mother your own
precious home—don't abandon me here
alone, helpless, living in the misery
you see, and more you've only heard of!   530
I won't be in your way!

                    It puts you out
I know, a cargo like me, but put up with it
anyway. You're *noble*, you *despise* meanness,
to you decency is *honorable*. But leave me
here? your name will be covered with shame!
My son, the glory's all yours if you
return me alive to Oita. Do it, it won't take
hardly a day, stow me wherever—
in the hold, by the prow, the stern—   540
wherever's least noxious to the crew.

O say you will! My boy, by the grace of Zeus
look at me! on my knees, sick as I am, helpless,
a miserable cripple! Don't leave me outcast
here, where human footsteps are unheard-of.
Give me safe passage to your own homeland
or Chalkedon in Euboea. From there it's not
far to Oita, to rugged Trakhis, to the gorgeous
rolling Sperkheios—you can present me
to my most loving father. For a long time   550
now, I've been afraid he's passed on.
I kept sending messages with those

who happened through, begging him
come alone with a ship. Take me home!
But maybe he's dead. Or the messengers
thought no more of it, and hurried
their own way home.

        You now, you're not just
a messenger, you're my escort—*you* take me.
Have mercy! Save me! You see how we all   560
live on the edge, with disaster a step away.
And the man who's doing well, he above all
should watch out for what *just like that*
will destroy his life.

CHORUS

(severally)

            Sir, pity him.
            He's told all
        the sufferings he has struggled with,
        not to be wished on any friend of mine.

        Sir, if you hate the hateful sons of Atreus—
            if it were me I'd turn   570
            their evils to his advantage—
        take him aboard your swift, well-rigged ship
            to the home he's homesick for,
            and escape the wrath of the gods.

NEOPTOLEMOS

      Careful.
It's easy to be easy-going . . . now. Yet
when you've lived awhile with his disease
you may disown your own words.

LEADER

Never. You will never, with justice,
accuse me of that.   580

NEOPTOLEMOS

I'd be ashamed if you seemed readier
than me to help him out. But if
that's what you want, let's sail. Quickly!
We should get a move on. The *ship*
won't turn him away. Just pray
the gods get us safely out of here,
wherever we're going.

PHILOKTETES

O glorious day! My dear friend! kind
sailors! if only I could *do* something
to prove how grateful I am to you!   590
Let's go, my boy—after we say good-bye
to the home that's not a home, inside.
You'll know then how I lived, and what
heart it took to survive. Just seeing it
anyone else would've given up. Out of
necessity, in time, I learned to live with it.

PHILOKTETES and NEOPTOLEMOS turn to enter the cave.

LEADER

      Wait! Hold on.
Two men coming—a shipmate with a stranger.
Before you go in, hear what they have to say.

MERCHANT (disguised Sailor) and another of Odysseus's Sailors appear.

MERCHANT

Son of Achilles? I asked this fellow here—   600
he with two others guarding your ship—
where I'd find you. Not that I expected
to come across you. I just . . . happened by!
Mine's the usual merchant ship, small crew,
returning home from Troy to the great vineyards
of Peparethos. On hearing these were *your* sailors
I decided not to sail away quietly—not without
giving you my news . . . and getting a reasonable
reward. I figured you know next to nothing
about your own affairs—new plots the Greeks   610
are mounting against you. Not idle talk
but actual doings already in the works.

NEOPTOLEMOS

Really, sir, that's thoughtful of you. If
I'm not unworthy of this, I'll remember you
with gratitude. But what 'doings'? What
exactly are the Greeks scheming against me?

MERCHANT

Old Phoinix and the sons of Theseus
are coming after you. In fully manned ships.

NEOPTOLEMOS

To force me back? Or talk me into it?

MERCHANT

I don't know. I'm just saying what I heard.   620

NEOPTOLEMOS

Are Phoinix and his crew so anxious
to get in good with the sons of Atreus?

MERCHANT

Believe it, they're on their way. Right now.

NEOPTOLEMOS

Odysseus couldn't sail himself, carrying
his own message? Is he afraid to?

MERCHANT

Just as I was weighing anchor
he and the son of Tydeus were setting out
after someone else.

NEOPTOLEMOS

Who? Odysseus himself after *what* someone?

MERCHANT

There was a man who, ah . . .   630
but first, who *is* that over there?
and keep your voice down.

NEOPTOLEMOS

Sir, you're looking at the famous Philoktetes.

MERCHANT

Then that's all you're getting from me.
Better haul yourself out of here. Now.

PHILOKTETES

What's he saying, boy? What's
your business, you two, haggling
in dark whispers over me?

NEOPTOLEMOS

I'm not sure yet. Whatever, he has to say it
openly, in the light, for everyone to hear.   640

MERCHANT

Son of Achilles, don't report me to the Greek army
for saying what I shouldn't! I'm a poor man, I get by
doing them favors. And getting a little something back.

NEOPTOLEMOS

The sons of Atreus hate me! And as *he* hates them,
that man is my best friend. Now you, coming here
with friendly intentions—you must tell us *everything*.

MERCHANT

Watch yourself. Young man.

NEOPTOLEMOS

I always have. And do so now.

MERCHANT

I'll hold you responsible.

NEOPTOLEMOS

Do that. Now talk.   650

MERCHANT raises his voice.

MERCHANT

OK. Right. . . . It's *this* man
those two are sailing after. The son of Tydeus
        and Lord Odysseus.
They swore they'd bring him in—by talking him into it
or by strong-arm arrest. All the Greeks heard Odysseus
say this, loud and clear. He was more sure of himself
than his partner was.

NEOPTOLEMOS

But why now? What moved the sons of Atreus
to think about this man? Years ago
        they threw him out!   660
What now has possessed them? The gods
demanding payback for their evil deeds?

MERCHANT

I'll tell you. Surely you haven't heard.
There was a seer, noble, a son of Priam
named Helenos. He was out and around
one night, alone, when wily Odysseus
(the creepy one none has a good word for)
caught him, chained him, and paraded him
before the Greeks. A prize catch.
Whatever they asked, Helenos had   670
a prophecy for. He said they'd never sack Troy
with its towers—unless they could persuade
this man to leave this island here and
bring him back. Right then Odysseus swore
he'd take him back and show him off
to the Greeks. He expected the man would come
willingly—if not, he'd be forced—and that if he,
Odysseus, failed, anyone who wanted his head
could have it. That's the whole story, young man.
You best get going now. You, and anyone   680
you care for.

PHILOKTETES

That bottomless pit of a man!
                  He'd persuade *me*
back to the Greeks? That will be the day
I'm dead. He can persuade me to rise
out of Hades into the light of day,
like his own father did.

MERCHANT

I know nothing of all that, but . . . .
good luck! Got to ship out now!
Gods be with you!   690

MERCHANT and Sailor leave.

PHILOKTETES

Horrifying, my boy, isn't it? The son of Laertes
dreams he'll sweet-talk me onto his ship,
lead me ashore, and show me off to the Greeks?
No way! I'd sooner listen to my deadliest enemy,
the snake that made my foot into a *thing*. Still
there's nothing *that* one wouldn't say or do,
and he'll be here soon!
                      Come on, son,
let's get going—put a stretch of open sea
between his ship and us. Go let's go!   700
Making good speed at the right time means
we can rest when the work is over.

NEOPTOLEMOS

In time. The wind's against us.
When it lets up, we'll go.

PHILOKTETES

Escaping evil, it's always good sailing.

NEOPTOLEMOS

Sure, but the wind's against *them*, too.

PHILOKTETES

To pirates looking for plunder
no wind is an ill one.

NEOPTOLEMOS

Well, if you insist, let's go—soon as you get
whatever you need or want from in there.   710

PHILOKTETES

A few things I need. Out of so very little.

NEOPTOLEMOS

What do you need that's not already on board?

PHILOKTETES

A certain herb. To tame this vicious wound.

NEOPTOLEMOS

Then get it out here. What else?

PHILOKTETES

Stray arrows I maybe overlooked.
Wouldn't want anyone else to get
their hands on them.

NEOPTOLEMOS

                    Is that really
the famous bow you have there?

PHILOKTETES

The one and only. This, in my hand.   720

NEOPTOLEMOS

May I take a closer look? Hold it?
Honor it as I would . . . a divine power?

PHILOKTETES

My boy, whatever's good for you,
anything I can give you, I will.

NEOPTOLEMOS

I'd love to touch it, but only—if the gods
think it right. Otherwise never mind.

PHILOKTETES

Son, as you're respectful, sure it's right.
It's you who put the gleam of sunlight
back into my eye—the hope of seeing
Oita again, my old father and friends—   730
you who, from under my enemies' feet,
have raised me up beyond their reach!
Take heart. The bow is yours to touch
before you hand it back. Then, for your
kindness to me, you'll be able to say
you alone of all mortal beings

touched it! As I myself did that day
I got it, by doing something kind.

NEOPTOLEMOS

I don't regret I happened on you—and found
a friend! Whoever knows how to pay back   740
kindness with kindness is worth more,
friend, than any possession. Go in, please.

PHILOKTETES

I'll show you in. My sickness wants you
to stand by, and support me.

PHILOKTETES and NEOPTOLEMOS go into the cave.

CHORUS
(severally)

            I've heard, but never seen,
        how the man who tried to slip into
                Zeus' wife's bed
    was caught, and bound on a whirling wheel
                by Zeus himself—

            but I'd never seen nor heard of   750
        a man with awfuller fate than this,
        who conned no one, harmed no one,
    who lived on good terms with everyone—
                yet was punished worse
                than anyone deserves.

I'm stunned at how
being so desolate here
hearing nothing ever but pounding surf
he yet
clung to his wretched life.   760

He himself was his only neighbor,
unable to walk,
with no one near to hear him suffer
screaming agony, nor feel with him
the disease eating his flesh, draining away his blood,

no one
to help gather healing herbs
from the good earth
—whenever a fit came over him—
to ease the burning pus from his ulcerous foot,   770

but went this way and that,
when the disease let up,
like a child with no nursemaid to steady it,
crawling around anywhere for anything
that might help somehow,

not for the food men work for
by seeding the blessed earth
but only, as happened,
with arrows shot from his quick-killing bow
he got food to eat.   780

A rotten life.

Ten years, and not one savoring taste of wine,

just

winding round toward any stagnant pool

he could find.

As PHILOKTETES and NEOPTOLEMOS are about to emerge from the cave . . .

LEADER

But now, after all that, he'll arrive at greatness

and a happy end. He's lucked out,

having met face to face the son of good people

who, in the fullness of so many moons, cutting across the sea

will bring him to his own   790

ancestral home

where Melian nymphs linger by the Sperkheios,

CHORUS

where bronze-shielded Herakles

rose in flames nearer the gods

amidst the lightning crashes of his father Zeus

high above Oita.

NEOPTOLEMOS and PHILOKTETES, with herbs and arrows, emerge.

NEOPTOLEMOS

Come on . . .

What's wrong? Why so awful still all of a sudden?

PHILOKTETES

(swallowing his agony)

Unh . . . Unh . . . Unh . . .

NEOPTOLEMOS

What's the matter?   800

PHILOKTETES

Nothing, nothing. Keep going, son.

NEOPTOLEMOS

You in pain? The usual?

PHILOKTETES

No, no. Think 's getting better . . .

                              Good gods!!

NEOPTOLEMOS

Then why the groaning? Why call on the gods?

PHILOKTETES

So they'll come . . . make better.

Gd! gd!

NEOPTOLEMOS

What's got *in*to you? Speak! say something!
I know something's wrong.

PHILOKTETES

Son I've had it. I can't hide the pain from you *o*   810
gods it runs right through me through me I'm
miserable *damn* done for! It's eating me alive!
          Son, I'm gone!
Buhh Bbuhh Buhhppuhpppuhppppuh
O for the gods you have a sword handy
          at hand?? USE IT!
Cut the heel OFF *now* now, no mind my life!
Quick son quick quick!

NEOPTOLEMOS

What? Why all of a sudden now?
what's new   820
all this screaming and hollering?

PHILOKTETES

You know.

NEOPTOLEMOS

What?

PHILOKTETES

My boy, you know.

NEOPTOLEMOS

Know what? What *is* the matter with you?

PHILOKTETES

You *have* to know! *Agaahh   Agaaahhh*

NEOPTOLEMOS

Your disease. It's unbearable.

PHILOKTETES

Unbearable beyond words. *Pityme!*

NEOPTOLEMOS

What should I do?

PHILOKTETES

Don't let me down,   830
don't be afraid—
this wandering disease
comes to me
when it's tired wandering,
and having had enough
it goes away.

NEOPTOLEMOS

Luckless man. Every misery there is
shows through you.
        Should I hold you?
Give you a helping hand?   840

PHILOKTETES

No, don't touch! But take the bow, please,
like you asked to—watch it till the pain

goes away. Guard it. I'll pass out asleep
when the fit passes, have to, or the pain
won't leave. Yet let me sleep in peace.
And if those men come, by the gods above
I beg you, don't give them or anyone else
the bow, willingly or unwillingly, or you'll
destroy yourself and kill me. Begging you.

NEOPTOLEMOS

Don't worry. This passes into no hands but yours   850
and mine. Give it here. And with it, good luck!

PHILOKTETES

Here, son, take it. Pray the gods don't envy
you—so the bow won't destroy you the way
it did me, and him who owned it before me.

NEOPTOLEMOS

Gods, give us this! Make it so we sail
with a swift following wind wherever
the heavens send us and our mission ends.

PHILOKTETES

          My boy, I'm afraid
you're praying for nothing. Look!
new dark blood oozing out   860
from somewhere deep,
dripping red again. I expect
a fresh worse attack. *Oooo*
          my foot

you excruciate me! The pain
slithers up, near, here! *Oooo*
        OoooOooo
NOW you know! Don't go! O
*Oooo*dysseus my friend if only this
        agony!   870
could stickstab through you
godgodgod
my generals general menelaos
general agamemnon if only
your flesh fed this sickness
as long as mine has
        AAHHHHZZ!
Death Death every day I beg you
what's keeping you
why don't you come?   880

My boy, you're a good boy
whyn't you
pick me up burn me in that fire out there,
        Lemnian fire,
I did the same for Herakles, son of Zeus,
for that I got the arms
you have there now. What say. What
        say, speak!
Why so quiet? Where are you?

NEOPTOLEMOS
Here, a long time here, heartsick   890
over your crushing pain.

PHILOKTETES

No, be brave *too*, my boy. The thing drops in
quickly yet goes quick too. Just please don't
leave me here alone.

NEOPTOLEMOS

Don't worry. We'll stay with you.

PHILOKTETES

You will?

NEOPTOLEMOS

Absolutely.

PHILOKTETES

Not that I'd ask you to swear to that, my boy.

NEOPTOLEMOS

Don't worry. It's not right to leave without you.

PHILOKTETES

Your hand on that! Give it.   900

NEOPTOLEMOS

I promise. We'll stay.

PHILOKTETES

Now. Up there. Take me.

NEOPTOLEMOS

What? Where there?

PHILOKTETES

(eyes rolling back into his head)

                    Up up . . .

NEOPTOLEMOS

(grabbing PHILOKTETES' arm)

Another fit? Why're you looking up . . . the *sky*?

PHILOKTETES

Let go me! Let go!

NEOPTOLEMOS

To go where?

PHILOKTETES

Let me go!

NEOPTOLEMOS

I won't.

PHILOKTETES

You'll kill me holding me like that.   910

NEOPTOLEMOS

(releases him)

OK OK. Now that you've calmed down.

PHILOKTETES

O Earth, take my dying body.
I can't stand up under this pain.

PHILOKTETES sinks to the earth.

NEOPTOLEMOS

I think . . . sleep will grip him soon. Look!
his head jerked back! His whole body's soaked
in sweat . . . the dark blood of a burst vein
trickling from his heel . . . Let's leave him
in peace, friends, so he can sleep.

CHORUS

Sweet sleep that feels no agony, no pain,
we pray you: kindly come   920
breathing your blessings, blessings
spread gently over him—
hold in his eyes this most serene glow
lowered on them now,
O lord of healing.
Come.

PHILOKTETES sleeps.

LEADER

Young man, you see the situation,
think where we're at.
What's the next move? Why don't we make it?

The Right Moment is everything!   930
When you see an opening you take it
quickly! That's the way to victory!

NEOPTOLEMOS
(raising his voice)
Sure, he doesn't hear a thing. But we've tracked him down
for what?—if we got the bow and sailed off, yet left him behind?
He's the victory trophy. It's him the gods want brought back.
We'd be shamed bragging of a job half done. Worse, done by lies!

CHORUS
(severally)
My boy, the gods will take care of that.
But when you speak next keep it down, *shsh*, down
to a whisper—
sick men sleep sleepless, they pick up on things.   940

So please, *whatever* you have to do
to achieve what you have in view
do it quietly
because if you keep on like this after this
—you know, doing what you're thinking—
a wise person can expect something real bad happening.

But now, my boy, the wind
the wind is right! The man lies

                blind, helpless, warmed into sleep
                     as though under cover of night.   950
                He can't get a hand or foot to do anything!

    Strengthless he is, like one laid at the edge of Hades.

LEADER

                Careful now. What are you thinking to do?
                          Timing is all.
                As far as I can figure, it's safest to move
                     quickly, without warning.

NEOPTOLEMOS

Shush! Watch it! His eyes
are open. He's raising his head.

PHILOKTETES

                     Ah, sun,
taking up where sleep leaves off!   960
I never dreamed to hope these
strangers would keep watch for me.
I dared not even think it.
You're so patient, son, so feeling
to stand by me in my agonies
helping me. Those O so brave
commanders, the sons of Atreus,
didn't have it in them
to put up with this. But you, you're
naturally noble! It's your bloodline.   970

You weren't fazed by my screaming
pain, or the putrid smell.

      But now
the disease has left this little lull
of peace, easing off the pain—so
come, my boy, help me, get me
back on my feet.
When the wooziness goes
we'll head for the ship
and quick, get under way.   980

NEOPTOLEMOS

I would not have believed it. What
a relief! You're up, your eyes open
looking around, and no pain! It's more
than I'd hoped for. After all that agony
your sleep looked like death.

Come, get up now. If you want, these men
can carry you. They won't begrudge the job,
seeing you and I are in this together.

PHILOKTETES

Thank you, son. You help me up, will you,
like you said? Don't bother the men.   990
I wouldn't want them weighed down by this
awful stench *too* soon. When we're living aboard
the ship, they'll have enough to put up with.

NEOPTOLEMOS

Come, stand up. Grab hold of me.

PHILOKTETES

Don't worry. I'm well used to getting myself up.

NEOPTOLEMOS

(to himself, helping PHILOKTETES up)
Damn! What *now* am I to do!?

PHILOKTETES

What's up, my boy? Where're you getting at?

NEOPTOLEMOS

I'm running on. I don't know where I'm going.

PHILOKTETES

"Don't know where" why? Don't talk that way.

NEOPTOLEMOS

But it's where I feel I'm at. This impasse!   1000

PHILOKTETES

My disease disgusts you? You've had
second thoughts about having me on board!?

NEOPTOLEMOS

Everything's *disgust* when a man steps outside
his breeding. And does what's beneath him.

PHILOKTETES

Helping an honorable man you don't do
anything your own father wouldn't say or do.

NEOPTOLEMOS

I'll be seen as dishonorable. That's
what's been tearing me apart.

PHILOKTETES

Not for what you're *doing*!
It's your *words* that worry me.   1010

NEOPTOLEMOS

Zeus, what will I do? Expose myself
as a traitor, by saying nothing? And yet
again, for telling the shameful truth?

PHILOKTETES

(as though to himself)
Unless I've got it all wrong, this person here
will betray and abandon me. And sail away.

NEOPTOLEMOS

Abandon, no. But take you on a voyage
so bitter . . . it's been tearing me up inside.

PHILOKTETES

What are you saying, my boy? I don't follow you.

NEOPTOLEMOS

I'll hide nothing. You must sail with us
to Troy, to the Greek forces,   1020
and serve under the sons of Atreus.

PHILOKTETES

What! What are you saying!?

NEOPTOLEMOS

Don't go moaning yet! You don't know the rest of . . .

PHILOKTETES

       WHAT now?
What do you mean to do to me?

NEOPTOLEMOS

Save you from this misery—then, together
we'll lay waste the plains of Troy.

PHILOKTETES

That's your plan? Really?

NEOPTOLEMOS

       It's a matter of utmost . . .
necessity. Don't get mad hear me out.   1030

PHILOKTETES

I'm done for! Betrayed! You, stranger, why
do this to me? The bow! Give it *back* to me!

NEOPTOLEMOS

Can't. Have to do what's right. And for
my own good, obey commanders' orders.

NEOPTOLEMOS, face averted, stands holding the bow.

PHILOKTETES

You scorched earth you terror monster
you filthy piece of work! What
have you done to me? you played me!
Ashamed to look me in the face, me
kneeling at your feet, heartless bastard?
Taking my bow you took my life!   1040
Give it back, *please*, give it, I beg you, boy!
By the gods of your fathers, don't steal
this it's my life!

       . . . Says
nothing. Looks away like
he'll never give it up.

       O you bays, you headlands,
you sheer rockface, you wild animals roaming the hills
with me, it's *you* I speak to—who else is there?—to you
only I wail what the son of Achilles, this boy,   1050
has done to me. He swore he'd bring me home?
He hauls me to Troy. And with his right hand
having given his word, he grabs and holds
my sacred bow, the bow of Herakles, son of Zeus,
to show off to the Greeks like it's his own.

Me too he drags off, as if he'd brought down
a big powerful man. He can't see he's killing
a carcass, a shadow of ghosting smoke.
Had I my strength he wouldn't have taken me.
Even as is he wouldn't, if he hadn't tricked me.   1060
But he did. Now what can I do?
      HAND IT BACK!
It's not too late! You can still step back
inside your own true self!

What say? What's that? Silence?

That's it then. I'm nothing.

O rock tunnel, again I go back
into you. Disarmed, stripped
of the means to live, my life
will wither away in loneliness.   1070
No bird on the wing, no animal
browsing the hills will I kill
with that bow there. I'll be food
for those who fed me, hunted
by those I myself hunted.
      Aaaa . . .
then will I give my blood back
for the blood of those I've killed—
victim, me, of one who seemed
to know no evil. *Die you!* But   1080
(directly at NEOPTOLEMOS)
not yet. Not till I see if you change

your mind again. If not, may you
die a rotten death.

CHORUS

What will we do, lord? It's up to you.
Set sail? Or do as he says?

NEOPTOLEMOS

For him, I feel. Not this moment
only, but for some time now.

PHILOKTETES

Pity, my boy, for love of the gods! Don't
give men grounds to despise you
for deceiving me.   1090

NEOPTOLEMOS

What will I do? Better I'd never left Skyros
than come to so hard a place.

PHILOKTETES

It's not *your* shame! You learned this
from truly evil teachers. *They* sent you!
Let them do their own dirty work.
Sail away, but first—give me back my arms.

NEOPTOLEMOS

Men, what will we do?

ODYSSEUS jumps out from behind the rocks.

ODYSSEUS

> DO!?

Do what, traitor? You won't get back

> here   and   1100

give   me   that   bow?

Two Sailors emerge from behind ODYSSEUS.

PHILOKTETES

Who is that voice? Odysseus!?

ODYSSEUS

Odysseus for sure. It's me myself you see.

PHILOKTETES

I've been sold out! It's *him* trapped me,
he stole my arms.

ODYSSEUS

Me, yes, me alone. My word on it.

PHILOKTETES

(to NEOPTOLEMOS)

The bow, son, give it back. Give me.

ODYSSEUS

He won't, never, even if he wants to.
And you'll come with it—or *these*

—ODYSSEUS gestures toward the Sailors—

will force you to.   1110

PHILOKTETES

You, you're the worst of the worst.
Them? Force *ME!?*

ODYSSEUS

If . . . you don't come quietly.

Burst of light, fading. Distant rumbling.

PHILOKTETES

O Lemnos—and you, O shooting flame
worked up by Hephestos—must I stand for this?
Let that man *drag* me off?

ODYSSEUS

Look here!
        it's ZEUS!
ZEUS rules here!
ZEUS decrees what happens!   1120
I carry out his orders.

PHILOKTETES

You're despicable. Hiding behind
your shield of lies and gods,
you make them liars, too.

ODYSSEUS

No, this is their truth.
This is the way we must go.

PHILOKTETES

No!

ODYSSEUS

Yes! You *must* submit.

PHILOKTETES

Then I'm damned! For sure my father

begot me not as a free man, but a slave.   1130

ODYSSEUS

No. You're the best among the best,

you're destined

to break Troy down into dust.

PHILOKTETES

Never! Whatever I suffer. Not while

I have these steep crags to stand on.

ODYSSEUS

And do what?

PHILOKTETES

Throw myself down, smash my head

on the rocks.

ODYSSEUS

(to Sailors)

Grab him! Both! Disable him!

Sailors hold PHILOKTETES.

PHILOKTETES

Poor bare hands, with no bow to draw,   1140
   hunted down now
together, held helpless under Odysseus . . .
(to ODYSSEUS*)*
As for you, you're the sort never has
a healthy or generous thought. Yet
sneaking up you've caught me out
again! hiding behind this boy stranger
who's too good for you, but for me
noble enough. All he'd thought to do
was what you wanted him to. Now he's
torn up over the terrible thing he did   1150
and the wrong done me. Your corrosive
soul, squinting out from some secret hole,
taught that boy what he didn't want to learn
—it wasn't in him—to be good at evil.

Now you want to tie me hand and foot,
take me from the same shore you cast me
up on—no friends, helpless, homeless—to live
my own death.
    Aie!
You should die! Out! I kept praying you would.   1160
But the gods leave nothing sweet for me. You,
you're happy to be alive. My pain is my life
lived among miseries, made a fool of
by the sons of Atreus you run errands for.

And yet, you sailed with them *only*
because you were tricked, and conscripted.
I, wretch, came on my own with seven ships
only to be dishonored, abandoned—for which
you blame them, and they blame you.

So why cart me off now? For what?   1170
I'm nothing. To you I'm a dead man.
Why's it now—for you, whom the gods
loathe—I'm not a stinking cripple?
How can you burn sacrifices to the gods
if I sail with you? How pour your offerings?
Wasn't that your excuse for dumping me here?

Die a rotten death, you! You'll have an awful end
if the gods love justice. And I'm sure they do—
because you wouldn't have sailed here
          looking for me   1180
if the gods hadn't driven you to it.

O gods of my fathers, O watchful ones,
when the time comes however late it comes
beat them all down, beat them, if you pity me.
My life is pathetic, but if I could see them
crushed, I could dream
I had been freed of my disease.

LEADER
A tough one, this stranger. Doesn't mince words,
Odysseus. He's not one to give in to misery.

ODYSSEUS

I'd have a lot to say back to him—if   1190
we had the time. For now all I'll say is
whatever the occasion, I'm the man for it.
If the times called for just and good, sure,
I could do that. As scrupulous as anyone.
But for me, in my very bones, victory is all.
Except now. With you.

                         For you, I'll back off.

(to the Sailors holding PHILOKTETES)

Yes! Let him go! Don't touch him. Let him
stay here. We've got your bow, we don't need you.
We have Teukros, an expert archer.   1200
And me. I can handle the bow as well as you
and damn well aim it, too. Who needs you?

        Good-bye!

Take a stroll around Lemnos. Enjoy yourself.

Sailors release PHILOKTETES.

                    Let's go.

Who knows? with this, your precious possession,
I may get the honors once meant for you.

PHILOKTETES

O gods, what will I do? You'll parade yourself
among the Greeks . . . showing off *my* bow?

ODYSSEUS

That's enough out of you! I'm going.   1210

PHILOKTETES

Son of Achilles! You, too? Without
a word for me, you'd leave?

ODYSSEUS

(to NEOPTOLEMOS)

Let's go! Don't even look. You being so
       noble and good
you'll spoil our good luck.

PHILOKTETES

(to CHORUS)

You too, strangers? You'd leave me all alone?
Have you no pity?

LEADER

The young man is our master. What he says, we say.

NEOPTOLEMOS

(to CHORUS)

The chief there will say I'm too soft, but you men
stay here, if that's what this one wants, for as long   1220
as it takes the sailors to set the rigging and get
everything shipshape. Until we've said our prayers
to the gods. By then maybe this one will think
better of us.

(to ODYSSEUS)

    All right let's go. The two of us.

(to CHORUS)

    You, when we call, come running.

ODYSSEUS and NEOPTOLEMOS leave.

PHILOKTETES

Then

O my deep hollow in the rock

—sun baked, icy cold—

I could never leave you after all!   1230

It's you will witness my death

o gods o gods

O forlorn space, all echoed up

reeking with my pain.

What now will befall my days?

Where will I find hope

—in my misery—of finding food?

You timid doves,

once so fearful,

fly freely in the whistling winds   1240

I can't stop you now!

LEADER

Your lot is hard, but *you*

you brought this damnation

down yourself *on* yourself,

unfortunate man. Know this.

Nothing outside you,
no overwhelming power
did—but you alone.
You had the chance
to choose a better way   1250
and chose a worse one.

PHILOKTETES

                    I'm miserable rotten miserable then—
                            abused in my misery
              I have to live with this, with no human being
                            other! Ever! How will I
                            get food? when I can't,
                        with my strong hands, let
                        the feathered arrows fly.

                    Sly words of a swindling soul
                                unsuspected   1260
                            wormed into me.
                May I see the one behind this scheme
                    suffer like me, and as long!

LEADER

It was the gods doomed
this on you, not me. I had
no hand in tricking you.
Aim your hate your curses
elsewhere. What I don't want
is you refusing my friendship.

PHILOKTETES

Aie me . . .   1270

somewhere, sitting on the shore

of the gray sea

he mocks me—showing off the weapon I lived by,

that none other ever handled.

Beloved bow

torn from hands that cared for you

if you have feelings feel for this

friend to Herakles.

He'll never use you again.

You're in the grasp of a new master,   1280

a crafty one: you will see

countless shameful deceptions rising in the face

of him, my enemy,

by whom a thousand awful things

O Zeus

were done to me.

LEADER

You're right to say what's right.

But once you've said it,

stop. Don't go on and on

needling and bitter.   1290

Odysseus was doing a job

the whole army wanted done,

doing what was best for all

them, in the long run.

PHILOKTETES

All you wingèd ones I've hunted,
all you tribes of glare-eyed beasts
feeding in the hills up here,
don't flee your nests or dens! Nor me!
I no longer hold the powerful bow
protecting me.   1300
Go where you want. I'm no threat now.
Get your own back, blood for blood,
glut yourselves much as you want
on my rotting flesh.

I'll die soon.
How will I find means to live?
Who lives on air without
all that life-giving earth gives?

*PHILOKTETES **heads back toward his cave.***

LEADER

By the gods, if you respect anything
respect a stranger who entreats you.   1310
Meet him halfway! It's up to you
to help yourself out of this fate.
It's pitiful the way this sickening
doom keeps eating away at you.
All the time in the world cannot
teach your body to live with this.

PHILOKTETES

       AGAIN

you bring old agony up!

You, the kindest of all

who've come ashore here.   1320

Why have you killed me like this?

What have you done to me?

CHORUS

(individual)

What do you mean?

PHILOKTETES

You planned to take me

back to Troy, which I hate.

CHORUS

(individual)

We think it's for the best.

PHILOKTETES

Then leave me. Now!

LEADER

Fine by us. More than glad to oblige.

(to the CHORUS)

Come on, let's take up

our stations on the ship.   1330

The CHORUS starts to leave.

PHILOKTETES
Please! As Zeus hears curses . . . Don't go.

LEADER
Get hold of yourself.

PHILOKTETES
Strangers! Wait! By the gods, I beg you!

LEADER
What is it?

PHILOKTETES
Doom! it's the doom got me.
Foot, damned foot, where ahead
can I *go* with you!?
Strangers! Come back!

Again the CHORUS has moved to leave.

LEADER
To do what *now* any different
from what you wanted before?   1340

PHILOKTETES
No sense getting angry at a man
so wild with pain he talks crazy.

CHORUS

(individual)

Unhappy man. Like we said, come with us.

PHILOKTETES

No! Never! Believe it. Not though
the lord of lightning bolts thunder
burn me up in his fire. Let Troy
die, die every man under its walls
who had the heart to cast out
this poor cripple of a foot.

But, strangers, one thing I pray you . . .   1350

CHORUS

(individual)

What thing?

PHILOKTETES

       A sword.
You have one at hand? Or ax?
Any weapon. Give it me.

CHORUS

(individual)

To do what?

PHILOKTETES

Hack this body limb from flesh

and *off* my head. Death is
death all I can think now.

CHORUS
(individual)
Why?

PHILOKTETES
So I can find my father.   1360

CHORUS
(individual)
Where?

PHILOKTETES
          In Hades.
No longer here, in the light.
O city of my fathers, if only
I could see you—fool as I was,
leaving your sacred streams
to help the Greeks, my enemies.
Only to come to . . . nothing

PHILOKTETES drags his foot back into the cave.

LEADER
I'd be gone back to the ship by now
if I hadn't seen Odysseus, and the son of Achilles,   1370
climbing this way.

NEOPTOLEMOS appears, dogged by ODYSSEUS.

ODYSSEUS

At least, would you be so *kind* as to say *why*
you're headed back here in such a hurry!

NEOPTOLEMOS

To undo the wrong I did. Back here.

ODYSSEUS

What kind of talk is that? What 'wrong'?

NEOPTOLEMOS

Obeying orders from you and the Greek army I . . .

ODYSSEUS

. . . did what? *What* that was beneath you?

NEOPTOLEMOS

I set a man up. Tricked him, and betrayed him.

ODYSSEUS

What man? You're not planning something *rash*, are you?

NEOPTOLEMOS

Rash? No. But to the son of Poias I'll . . .   1380

ODYSSEUS

. . . what!? You'll what?
I feel strange uneasiness creeping up on me.

NEOPTOLEMOS

I'll . . . give him the bow back.

ODYSSEUS

By Zeus you can't mean that! Not *really* give it back?

NEOPTOLEMOS

Really. I got it by fraud. I have no right to it.

ODYSSEUS

Gods above! You're just giving me a hard time, right?

NEOPTOLEMOS

Only if truth gives you a hard time.

ODYSSEUS

What do you mean? Son of Achilles, what are you saying?

NEOPTOLEMOS

How many times do I have to go over this? Two? Three?

ODYSSEUS

Better you hadn't 'gone over' in the first place.   1390

NEOPTOLEMOS

Well relax. Now you've heard it all.

ODYSSEUS

There's someone will stop you from doing this.

NEOPTOLEMOS

Meaning what? Who's to stop me?

ODYSSEUS

The whole Greek army. Me with them.

NEOPTOLEMOS

Smart as *you* are, your words aren't.

ODYSSEUS

There's nothing smart in what you say *or* do.

NEOPTOLEMOS

Being *just* beats being 'smart.'

ODYSSEUS

How is it just to give up what you got
thanks to my . . . strategic advice?

NEOPTOLEMOS

I did something shameful. I have to undo it.   1400

ODYSSEUS

You're not afraid what the Greeks will do
to *you*, if you do that?

NEOPTOLEMOS

With justice by my side, I'm not afraid.

ODYSSEUS

You will be.

NEOPTOLEMOS

I won't back off. Even for you.

ODYSSEUS

We won't fight the Trojans then. But you.

NEOPTOLEMOS

If it comes to that, so be it.

ODYSSEUS

(reaching)

     You see my right hand?
By my sword hilt?

NEOPTOLEMOS

(reaching)

     Watch my own, it's   1410
quick as yours.

ODYSSEUS

(withdrawing his hand)

OK. I'm not bothering with you anymore.
I'll go tell the whole army about this.
They'll straighten you out.

ODYSSEUS leaves. Downhill, he hides behind rocks.

NEOPTOLEMOS

(partly to himself, as ODYSSEUS is hurrying off)

    Good thinking!

If you stay this sensible you might even

keep yourself out of trouble.

NEOPTOLEMOS turns to face the mouth of the cave.

NEOPTOLEMOS

But you, son of Poias, Philoktetes,

come out from your rocky enclosure!

PHILOKTETES

(from within)

What's all the racket out there? Strangers,   1420

why are you calling? What do you want from me?

PHILOKTETES emerges, surprised. He had expected only sailors.

O no. Not good. You here to announce

new bad news, on top of my other miseries?

NEOPTOLEMOS

Don't be afraid. Hear what I have to say.

PHILOKTETES

That scares me. Last time I believed

your reassuring words, I got taken.

NEOPTOLEMOS

But can't I change my mind? Again?

PHILOKTETES

Just how you talked when you stole my bow.
So trustworthy. Friendly. And treacherous.

NEOPTOLEMOS

Not now though. All I want to know is: 1430
you aim to hold on here, or sail with us?

PHILOKTETES

       Stop! Enough!
Whatever you say, you're wasting your breath.

NEOPTOLEMOS

Your mind's made up?

PHILOKTETES

More than words can say. Yes.

NEOPTOLEMOS

I wish I could have brought you round on this,
but . . . if my words are getting nowhere, I quit.

PHILOKTETES

       Right. You're getting nowhere.
I'll never feel friendly toward you. Now, after
stealing by deceit the bow that means my life,   1440

you come to give advice? The shameless son
of a noble father!? Die! the bunch of you,
sons of Atreus, Odysseus son of Laertes,
and you!

NEOPTOLEMOS

Stop! Enough!
No more curses. Here. Take them.

NEOPTOLEMOS offers PHILOKTETES the bow and arrows.

PHILOKTETES

What *are* you saying! This another trick?

NEOPTOLEMOS

No, I swear. By the awesome majesty
of Zeus on high.

PHILOKTETES

Wonderful words! If true.   1450

NEOPTOLEMOS

The act speaks for itself. Hold out your right hand,
take these. They're yours.

NEOPTOLEMOS hands weapons to PHILOKTETES.

VOICE OF ODYSSEUS

The gods be my witness . . .

ODYSSEUS jumps out from behind rocks.

          I FORBID THIS! By authority
of the sons of Atreus and the entire Greek army!

PHILOKTETES
My boy . . . whose voice . . . I hear *Odysseus*?

ODYSSEUS
Better believe it. Up close, too!
Me, see? The Odysseus who will
cart you off to the plains of Troy
by force, no matter what   1460
the son of Achilles wants.

PHILOKTETES
Not without paying for it . . .

—he has fitted an arrow to the bowstring and is drawing the bow back—

         if this arrow flies true.

NEOPTOLEMOS
(grabbing PHILOKTETES' arm)
By the gods, no! Don't let it go!

PHILOKTETES
Let go let go my hand dear boy!

NEOPTOLEMOS

No. I will not.

PHILOKTETES

       Why did you stop me
killing my enemy *he hates me* with my bow?

NEOPTOLEMOS

This killing isn't worthy of you. Nor of me.

ODYSSEUS has run off.

PHILOKTETES

Well one thing's sure. Greek army chiefs   1470
who trumpet themselves with bold words
are cowards at backing them up.

NEOPTOLEMOS

So let that be. You have your bow now.
No reason to be mad, or hold anything
against me.

PHILOKTETES

No, son, there isn't. You've shown
the stock you come from. Not Sisyphos
but Achilles, the noblest man who lived, and now
no less so among the dead.

NEOPTOLEMOS

I'm pleased, hearing you speak so well   1480
of my father, and of me. But now listen.

I have something to put to you.
                                    What fortunes
the gods give us, we have to live with.
But when, like you, we willfully *persist*
in being victims, there's no excuse for that.
No pardoning, no pity.
You're stubborn, like an animal. You won't
take advice. Someone says something helpful
you hate him. Like he's an enemy. Even so   1490
I'll speak up. May Zeus, god of oaths, witness.
Mark my words. Write them down in your heart.
Your sickness and pain are a doom from a god.
You came too close to the serpent you didn't see
guarding the open shrine of the god Chrysē.
You'll never find relief, not so long as this
sun rises in the east and sinks in the west,
till you come freely to the plains of Troy
and meet with the sons of Asklepios
who will cure you. With the bow then   1500
and with me, you will bring down Troy.

PHILOKTETES doesn't respond.

How do I know this will happen? I'll tell you.
We took a Trojan prisoner: Helenos, a prophet
as good as his word. He says straight out this
must happen. What's more, Troy must fall
this summer. If I lie, he says, then kill me.
                                    Now you know.
So come with us, freely. The bonus is,

your glory will grow! You'll stand out among
the Greeks—find healing hands—and when   1510
you've reduced Troy *the source of so many*
tears to ruins, you'll be famous.

PHILOKTETES

(quietly, as if speaking into a void)

Hateful life! why do you hold me
still above ground, in the daylight
of here on earth?
Why haven't you let me go
down into darkest Hades?

What will I do? How can I not
hear this man's well-meant advice?
Should I give in then? But how,   1520
after that, show myself in public,
shunned as I am? Who will speak to me?
And O my eyes, you've seen all
they've done to me, how could you
bear to see me going along with
the sons of Atreus who, here,
have made me rot away?
Or that damned son of Laertes?

It's not bitterness over the past
that eats at me, but what I expect   1530
these men will make me suffer
in days to come. Men whose souls
have conceived, once, an evil know

ever after how to breed other evils.

(to NEOPTOLEMOS)

You too I wonder at, wondering . . .
you yourself shouldn't be going to Troy,
you should keep me from going too!
Those men humiliated you, stripped you
of your father's arms—now you want
to join them? And make me join too?   1540

No, my boy, no. Take me home, like
you promised. And you, stay in Skyros.
Let these evil men die their evil death.
My father and I, both, will thank you
twice over. By not helping these evil
ones, you won't seem to be one yourself.

NEOPTOLEMOS

Reasonable words. Even so I wish
you'd trust the gods, trust my word,
and as a friend
sail with me away from here.   1550

PHILOKTETES

To Troy!? To the despicable sons
of Atreus? With this putrid foot?

NEOPTOLEMOS

To those who'll save you *and* your pus-running foot
from the pain of rotting away.

PHILOKTETES

Meaning what? What's behind *that* advice?

NEOPTOLEMOS

What I see ahead, if we do this, will be best
for both of us.

PHILOKTETES

Aren't you ashamed? Saying such a thing
the gods can hear?

NEOPTOLEMOS

What shame? I'm helping out a friend.   1560

PHILOKTETES

Helping out the sons of Atreus? Or me?

NEOPTOLEMOS

You, I should imagine. Speaking as your friend.

PHILOKTETES

How's that? If you'd turn me over to my enemies?

NEOPTOLEMOS

Seeing as you're down, sir, you shouldn't be so difficult.

PHILOKTETES

You'll do me in, I just know it . . . talking that way.

NEOPTOLEMOS

I won't, I'm telling you. You don't understand.

PHILOKTETES

Don't I know the sons of Atreus exiled me here?

NEOPTOLEMOS

They did. But now know how
they would save you!

PHILOKTETES

Never happen. Not if it means   1570
agreeing I'll go back to Troy.

NEOPTOLEMOS

What will I do then, if I can't convince you
of anything? Easier for me to shut up, and you
can live on as you are, with no way out.

PHILOKTETES

Let *me* suffer what's mine. But you
with your hand in mine promised
you'd bring me home. Now, my boy,
you have to keep that promise.
No more talk of Troy. I've had enough
of cryings and sorrows.   1580

NEOPTOLEMOS

That's what you want? . . . Let's go then.

PHILOKTETES

Nobly spoken!

NEOPTOLEMOS

(offering help)

Step by step, now. Careful.

PHILOKTETES

What I can, I'll do.

NEOPTOLEMOS

But how can I keep from being
blamed by the Greeks?

PHILOKTETES

Don't give that a thought.

NEOPTOLEMOS

I have to. Suppose they attack my country?

PHILOKTETES

I'll be waiting for them.

NEOPTOLEMOS

How can you help?   1590

PHILOKTETES

Herakles' bow. That's how.

HERAKLES appears on the rocks above them.

NEOPTOLEMOS

Meaning what?

PHILOKTETES

I'll make them keep their distance.

NEOPTOLEMOS

Then kiss this ground good-bye. We're going.

HERAKLES, still unnoticed by PHILOKTETES and NEOPTOLEMOS, steps nearer.

HERAKLES

Not yet! Not till you've heard
what *I* will say, son of Poias!

Startled, PHILOKTETES and NEOPTOLEMOS turn and look up.

The voice of Herakles, yes! and this
is his face. For you I've left
the heavens. To let you know
what Zeus plans—to keep you   1600
from going where you're going,
and get you to listen to me.

First, know my own story—how
after many ordeals I achieved
as you now see

the glory that is deathless.
It's certain your own sufferings
are destined to bring you, too,
to glory. Go with this man to Troy
where, first, you'll be cured of this   1610
horrible disease. The Greek army
will choose you as its foremost
warrior. With my bow you will
kill Paris, who began all this misery.
You will sack Troy and be honored
with the choicest spoils. Bring these
home with you to the Oitan highlands
to please your father, Poias. The other
spoils such as common soldiers get
lay on my funeral pyre: as a tribute   1620
to my bow.

(to NEOPTOLEMOS)

       This advice
goes for you, too, son of Achilles.
You're not strong enough to take Troy
without him. Nor he to take it without you.
You're like two lions prowling the same
grounds, each guarding the other.

(to PHILOKTETES)

       I'll send Asklepios
to Troy, to cure you of your disease,
for Troy is doomed to fall a second time   1630
beneath my bow. Yet remember, when
you sack Troy show piety toward all things

relating to the gods. To Zeus, nothing
matters more. The sacred doesn't die
when men do. Whether they live or die,
holiness endures.

PHILOKTETES

Voice bringing back so much
I've longed for! You showing yourself
after so many long years! *Your* words
I will not disobey.   1640

NEOPTOLEMOS

And I the same.

HERAKLES

Don't waste time then. Move.
The wind is fair and following.
The time to act is now.

HERAKLES vanishes.

PHILOKTETES

                Come then, just
let me pay my respects to the land
I'm leaving . . . . Good-bye, cave, you
that watched out with me. Good-bye
you nymphs of the marshy meadows,
and you, O low groaning ocean   1650
booming thunder spume

against the headland—where deep
within the cave, how often my head
was drizzled by gusts of southerly wind,
how often the Mount of Hermes broke
my own mournful echoes back,
storming me with my sorrows.

But now you springs, and you
Lycean well sacred to Apollo,
I'm leaving you, at long last   1660
leaving—

I had never dared hope
for this.

Good-bye, Lemnos, surrounded by sea:
set me free and uncomplaining
with smooth sailing where
a great destiny takes me
by the counsel of friends
and, above all, the god who
subduing everything   1670
has brought this to pass.

CHORUS
Let's all set off together
now, praying the nymphs of the sea
come take us safely home.

NOTES TO THE PLAY

NEOPTOLEMOS Son of Achilles. A neophyte, new to war
and to the world.

2 *Lemnos* Lemnos, as staged, is desolate, though historically
the island was inhabited. Here the fable-like setting, unclut-
tered by the lumber of insignificant descriptive detail, allows
the psychological and physiological drama to be projected
with near hallucinatory clarity. It deepens Philoktetes' iso-
lation from the world—cut off not only from human com-
panionship, but from human history. With Neoptolemos's
arrival, however, he is plunged back into the midst of both.

5–7 *as you're truly the son / of Achilles . . . listen to me* Odysseus uses Neoptolemos's pedigree as a 'hook' to enlist him
in a scheme that contradicts everything his breeding stands
for. (There's no "as" or "listen to me" in the Greek. This is a
framing device, signaling that Odysseus's studied identifica-
tion of Neoptolemos is not 'dead exposition' for an audience
needing background information. Rather, the passage has a
dramatic function that an ancient Greek audience, unlike a
modern one, would have recognized without prompting. It
is directed at Neoptolemos himself—to get him to associate
this questionable undertaking with the heroic legacy of his
father, Achilles.)

9 *the Malian, son of Poias* Philoktetes' lineage confirms his nobility. Malis is under Mount Oita, where Philoktetes, in an act of mercy, put the torch to Herakles' funeral pyre.

10 *under orders from the chiefs* Odysseus cites extenuating circumstances to explain away his past abandonment of Philoktetes. He was acting under orders. Philoktetes' odor and screams were unbearable to the army, they interfered with religious rituals, etc.

19–20 *my scheme / to take him is wasted* The Odysseus of the post–Homeric Epic Cycle, unlike the Odysseus of Homer, is known for his cunning and unscrupulousness. This negative portrayal extends into the classical era of Sophocles' own time. The exemplary Odysseus of *Aias*—who averts, if he does not resolve, the highly charged sociopolitical impasse dramatized in that play—is a rare exception.

21 *it's your job to help me carry this out* Odysseus, tightening his grip on Neoptolemos, lets the young man know he's not a fellow-warrior on a mission but a subordinate under military command.

50 *scrounging for food* The Greek phrase implies that Philoktetes forages for food more like an animal than a human being.

51 *Send your man to watch out* The unseen sailor who trailed them as they made their way up the cliff.

60 *Some plan you haven't heard yet* Having positioned Neoptolemos to do what he (thought he) would never do, Odysseus keeps drawing the young man in, by stages deepening his involvement.

65 *reach into his soul. / Take it!* A literal translation. This is well-designed to appeal to Neoptolemos. Even as it counters his putative ethic of always acting 'aboveboard,' rhetorically it is

pitched to his instinctive tendency, as a young and eager warrior, to *act*.

70 *they'd begged you, prayed you, to leave your home* "They" are Odysseus and Phoinix.

71 *you were their only hope of taking Troy* What Odysseus has not said, yet, is that as much as they need Neoptolemos, they also need Philoktetes and the bow given to him by Herakles.

74–75 *Instead / they handed them over to* Odysseus Cf. *Aias*.

81–82 You *didn't / come to Troy bound by an oath* Unlike Philoktetes, Odysseus did not go to Troy voluntarily. He and other suitors of Helen were bound by an oath to her father, Tyndareus, to help her husband (who has turned out to be Menelaos) if she were seduced or abducted by another man. When Helen went off with Paris, Odysseus did everything he could to avoid going to war. He pretended to be mad, harnessing a donkey and an ox—which have different stride lengths—to his plow. But when the Greeks put his young son Telemachus in front of the plow, Odysseus veered to save him, proving his sanity. The irony of Odysseus the conscript coming to dragoon Philoktetes, who had volunteered to fight in the war, is not incidental. Resolutions in this world, as in ours, are not necessarily nor even ordinarily based on what is fair or just. As mandated by Herakles, the demands of a temporal justice based on the individual must be set aside when the enduring good of the collectivity is at stake. What's more, this will benefit the individual as well. (e.g., The 'good' Odysseus in *Aias* insists that even though Aias has been an enemy, he should be given a proper burial. Because, as Odysseus says: "One day I will have the same need.")

90 *O . . . I know, it's not like you* Odysseus knows the still-green Neoptolemos inside out. That will change, however, as Neoptolemos, getting a 'crash course' experience of the world from Philoktetes, becomes more complex and less predictable.

94–95 *Give yourself . . . one short, shameless / stretch of day* Having drawn Neoptolemos this far in, rather than mask or excuse the shamelessness of the deception, Odysseus flaunts it—but speaks as though the shamelessness could be limited to the duration of the act itself.

96–97 *Then, forever after . . . the very soul of honor* A cynical rationale informed by considerable realism and truth. The capture of Troy could well 'put paid' any lingering sense of shame.

99–100 *It's not in me . . . in my father* Neoptolemos's certainty of his own rectitude comes not from experience but confidence in his breeding.

105–106 *I'd rather do / what's right, and fail* As Neoptolemos's idealistic, untested morality teeters amidst the complexity and confusion of life-in-the-world, his moral posture grows increasingly assertive and abstract.

110–111 *learned it's words / that move people, not deeds* A scholiast (an ancient interpreter of classical texts) identified this as a slander directed against contemporary Athenian politicians.

118 *Arrows definite as the death they deliver* Sophocles reproduces the Homeric tendency to 'personify' weapons as though they were self-acting. This short, sharp exchange between Odysseus and Neoptolemos is an instance of *stichomythia*, a technique for increasing dramatic intensity by assigning alternating lines or 'rows' of speech to two

characters, often with the alternating lines linked by a single word. (Neoptolemos: "Won't the *look* on my face give me away?" Odysseus: "*Look* to what's in it for you.")

122–123 *Not if lying gets us through this / dragged-out war* Literally, "Not if the lie brings deliverance." This is not about deliverance in general, however, but about breaking the specific impasse the Homeric Greeks have found themselves at. Fifth-century Greeks would have had that impasse (we'd use metaphors such as 'bogged down' or 'quagmire') firmly in mind. It's less likely that modern audiences will have a comparable awareness.

128 *not going to take Troy? Like you said?* Plural "you." Cf. 390–391.

135–136 *what I told you then? Understood? . . . I've said I would* This is the only place where Sophocles uses end rhyme to close off a passage of *stichomythia*. Odysseus is making sure that Neoptolemos understands not only what he's supposed to do, but its implications.

146–148 *May Hermes . . . Defender of Athens* Hermes, the god who speeds things along, is also associated with thievery and deception. Athena, the patron of Odysseus, is identified here as Athena Polias (the Defender of Athens). Sophocles invokes Athena's relationship to Athens to link *Odysseus* with Athens—thus reconceiving him, anachronistically, as a representative of the Athenian polity. Homer's Odysseus had no relation to 'the City.' This then is a critical political interpolation by Sophocles.

160–161 You, *still in youth, / have had this passed down to you* "The whole ancestral power of Achilles' family" is now in the hands of Neoptolemos (Webster, 80).

168–179 *If I signal you . . . cursed creature! Where is he?* The exceedingly green Neoptolemos is watched over by sailors older than he is. When he instructs them to help as best they can, the Chorus Leader reminds him that "we've been watching out for you / a long time, sir." And when they ask the present whereabouts of Philoktetes, known to be dangerous, Neoptolemos misses the point. Instead he dwells on obvious features of the immediate landscape, eliciting an exasperated outburst from the Leader. Neoptolemos may be the sailors' master, but he doesn't know which end is up. Folkish humor (e.g., lines 937–946, 1024–1028, *passim*) is crucial to the dramatic texture. With Philoktetes in agony at one moment, petulant the next, humor keeps the play from crossing over into melodrama. It also serves a strategic function. By loosening the reins of the plot, especially the highly emotional ups and downs, it conditions the audience to take Philoktetes' abrupt final turnabout more easily in stride.

187 *I feel sorry for him* Here the sailors feel for Philoktetes. Yet when he's lying helpless, they'll be eager to capture him. This doesn't mean they're self-contradictory or insincere. They feel what they're free to feel, or what their own interests compel them to feel, depending on what the moment and the circumstances allow for.

203 *dappled or shaggy beasts* Someone has remarked on Sophocles' "careful imprecision." The "beasts" could be spotted deer and shaggy goats, but we'll never know. Nor should we. We're not supposed to get caught up in such details. Sophocles, having another order of 'truth' in view, needs to keep the fabulous or otherworldly aspect of Lemnos— it's so *purely* what it is—intact.

206–208 *Echo . . . crying back at him his own crying* Rather than lessen his solitude, Echo compounds it.

211 *the vicious Chrysē* The serpent guarding the shrine of Chrysē, an obscure, localized deity, has bitten and infected Philoktetes. The gods allowed this to happen, but only to put off the destined fall of Troy until the time was right. Foreknowledge of this comes from Helenos, the Trojan seer captured by Odysseus.

214 *his almighty bow* The bow Herakles gave Philoktetes.

242 *this desolate island* In the plays (now lost) that Aeschylus and Euripides wrote about Philoktetes, the island was inhabited. The choruses were made up of Lemnians.

249 *if you really come as friends* Time and again Philoktetes' desperate hopes for deliverance are hedged by his own justifiable suspicions.

269 *your grandfather Lykomedes* Neoptolemos's grandfather on his mother's side.

281 *Not one word of me abandoned here* A crushing blow to his pride as a warrior.

287–288 *my disease / flourishes its worst, and spreads* As is typical of Philoktetes, he conceives his disease as having a life of its own.

293 *two commanders and Odysseus* The Greek text doesn't name Odysseus but refers to him by his title: Lord of Kephallenia. The island of Kephallenia was part of Odysseus's domain.

296–297 *vicious . . . vicious* The repetition occurs in the original text. The story itself needed no elaboration, as the audience would have been familiar with it.

298 *Sickness I was left alone with* Another 'personification,' or self-acting entity.

305–306 *some rags . . . Me too they left* Implicitly equating
    Philoktetes with the rags.

319–320 *I made do / myself. Had to.* Philoktetes is a lord, not a
    generic warrior. He was not prepared, emotionally or prac-
    tically, to live a 'make-do' life. His hands are made for his
    bow, not for menial nor craft work, e.g., his wooden cup is
    "rough, poorly made."

368 *You said it, boy!* "Philoktetes, excited by the boy's words,
    turns colloquial. The exclamation . . . does not recur [in the
    canon of classical tragedies]" (Ussher, 122).

387 *the great Odysseus* Sarcastic, in keeping with Odysseus's
    instructions to say "anything you want about me. Nothing's
    too nasty" (76).

395–396 *I wanted so to see my father / unburied* Neoptolemos,
    born the day Achilles left for Troy, has never seen his father.

397 *Then too, they promised me* Neoptolemos's ambition for
    success as a warrior never leaves him. Herakles in his part-
    ing words will allude to this.

401 *still painful Sigeion* "Painful" because it's where he first
    landed at Troy. The soldiers crowding round, swearing that
    in Neoptolemos "the dead Achilles lived again," brought
    home to him the *felt* reality of his father's death.

431–433 *An army, like a city, depends . . . from their lead-
    ers* Popular wisdom cast as a *gnōmē*, a moral aphorism or
    proverb. N.B. Homilies or 'old sayings' crop up from time to
    time, especially among the Chorus. The *dramatic* utility of
    this maxim, as distinguished from its substance, is that it's
    canned. It serves as a convenient device for Neoptolemos to
    put the minefield of his improvised story behind him—to seal
    it off with a truism, thus precluding further discussion or

questioning. As with any drama, it's necessary to recognize not only what is said, but what the saying is *doing*. In dramatic as in social context, even a cliché may reveal something having little or nothing to do with its ostensible meaning. This particular *gnōmē* may have an extratheatrical function as well. According to Jebb: "This play was brought out in the spring of 409 B.C. The Revolution of the Four Hundred in the summer of 411 B.C. was emphatically a case in which Peisander and his fellow oligarchs had corrupted or intimidated the polis. Thus, to the ears of an Athenian audience, [Sophocles'] verses might well suggest a lightly-hinted apology for those citizens who, against their will, had been compromised by the conspirators" (1898, 69–70). When we put all this together, Neoptolemos's patchwork 'saying' becomes rich soil indeed.

436–442 *Goddess of Mountains ... Wondrous Mother* The Chorus invokes a goddess who has the features of Mother Earth and Kybele, "a Phrygian goddess identified with the Greek Rhea, mother of Zeus" (Schein, 37). Effectively, the sailors, with their invocation of the goddess and their criticism of the sons of Atreus, are lending atmospheric support to Neoptolemos's deception.

467 *the bastard Sisyphos begot then sold to Laertes* Sisyphos was notorious for his cunning. Anticleia, made pregnant by Sisyphos, was carrying Odysseus when Laertes bought her with 'many gifts.'

471 *Nestor of Pylos* King of Pylos. His son, Antilochos, was a leading warrior and a friend of Achilles.

483 *Patroklos* Achilles' lover. He was killed by Hektor, who was in turn killed by Achilles.

487–488 *war doesn't single out evil men, but in general kills the good* A common saying.

493 *Thersites* An ugly, lame, quarrelsome man who reputedly taunted Achilles, who then killed him. In the *Iliad*, as a self-appointed representative of the *dêmos*, the common people, Thersites is a caricature. There he's pitted against Odysseus, who embodies the dominant monarchic/aristocratic order and perspective informing the *Iliad* (Cartledge, 33–37).

499–500 *keeping / the slick smooth ones out of Hades* e.g., Sisyphos.

507 *O son of an Oitan father* Reminder of Philoktetes' link to Herakles.

513 *rockbound Skyros* Neoptolemos's home island.

547 *Chalkedon in Euboea* A contemporary of Philoktetes' father, Poias.

570–571 *if it were me I'd turn / their evils to his advantage* Even as the Chorus gives Neoptolemos (sometimes impassioned) advice, the sailors are not about to press the matter. After all, he's still their master.

585–587 *Just pray . . . wherever we're going* The indefinition of Neoptolemos's "wherever" does double duty: it allows him to avoid being presumptuous, which would offend the gods, and it allows Philoktetes to persist in the delusion that they're going to take him home.

MERCHANT The charade orchestrated by Odysseus to hasten Philoktetes' departure from the island. In this play-within-a-play-within-a-play, the fake merchant speaks in a progressively 'confidential' tone, whereas Neoptolemos, playing to Philoktetes, grows louder and louder.

605–606 *vineyards / of Peparethos* A small island famous for its wine. The 'Merchant' supplies wine to the Greek forces at the siege of Troy. He'll peddle anything to anyone, wine or information, provided there's money in it. This gives the faux merchant an air of authenticity. Possibly it gave the audience a bit of extracurricular amusement as well.

617 *and the sons of Theseus* Theseus was the legendary founder of Athens. Akamas and Demophon, his sons, are obscure figures known mainly from post-Homeric poems about the sack of Troy. They do not appear in the *Iliad*. But then, *all* male Athenians are in a sense 'sons of Theseus.' This seemingly offhand allusion is one of many intimations or reminders that *Philoktetes* is, among other things—and especially as regards the ethos of Odysseus—also a comment on contemporary Athens.

630–631 *a man who . . . but first, who is that over there?* An interruption intended to rekindle Philoketes' fears and hasten his departure from Lemnos.

682 *That bottomless pit of a man* Literally, "that utter devil" (Ussher, 61) or "utter plague" (Lloyd-Jones, 315) or something on the order of "he's a complete loss" (Webster, 108). The Greek is an abusive phrase that Ussher (131) thinks may be colloquial, though it seems not to exist in Greek comedy. The problem is that ritual imprecations such as these can't be taken seriously. "Bottomless pit" is, then, a shot in the dark of Hades—which Odysseus's father, Sisyphos, had already tested to its limits (see below).

683–687 He'd *persuade* me . . . *to rise* . . . *like his own father did* The dying Sisyphos instructed his wife not to bury him. When he arrived in the underworld, he asked that Hades return him to earth—to punish her for not doing her duty and burying him. Hades consented, and Sisyphos returned to the world until fate in the guise of Necessity (*anangke*) put him under for good.

713 *To tame this vicious wound* Philoktetes regards the wound as a wild beast (Ussher, 132). That is, he objectifies the wound by 'animating' but *not* anthropomorphizing it. The wound remains 'other.' This is not so with personification as we ordinarily, and correctly, understand that term: as a means of appropriating or absorbing what is 'other,' or projecting that 'other' as an expression of one's self.

740–741 *Whoever knows how to pay back / kindness* A *gnōmē* or maxim.

746–747 *the man who tried to slip into / Zeus' wife's bed* As punishment for his grievous violation of the laws of hospitality, Ixion was bound forever to a wheel of fire.

790–791 *will bring him to his own / ancestral home* They feel for Philoktetes in his misery, yet embellish the deception that Neoptolemos will return him to his home in Oita.

793–796 *bronze-shielded Herakles / rose in flames . . . high above Oita* Cf. *Women of Trakhis.*

832 *this wandering disease* Literally, "wanderer": an ancient medical term for intermittent fever (Ussher, 136).

856–857 *wherever / the heavens send us* Again, Neoptolemos's piety hides his purposeful ambiguity. He knows full well where 'the heavens' are sending them.

869 *Oooodysseus, my friend* Odysseus is not named in the Greek text, where he's called "the Kephallenian."

884 *Lemnian fire* Mount Mosychlos, associated with Hephestos.

889 *Where are you?* Literally, "Where are you [in your thinking]?" The "where" is idiomatic, as in "Where're you at?" or "Where's your mind at?" Compare this with the exchange (997–1000) that begins when Philoktetes, troubled that a suddenly disoriented Neoptolemos has started talking to himself, asks: "Where're you getting at?" At that juncture the highly adaptable, idiomatic "where" metamorphoses into a revelatory road metaphor.

898 *Not that I'd ask you to swear to that* Philoktetes is not asking for a solemn oath but simply a "hand pledge" or handshake. Cf. 900: "Your hand on that! Give it."

902–904 *Now. Up there. Take me ... Up up ...* Apparently referring to the volcano, Mount Mosychlos. In his agony, Philoktetes wants, like Herakles, to be consumed by fire.

910 *You'll kill me holding me like that* This is resonant given Sophocles' hands-on involvement in medicine and practical health care. But the full implications of these words, their 'teaching message,' are not exhausted by their use in a medical context. Clearly, it is necessary but not sufficient to do the right thing. It must also be done *in the right way*. So Herakles, later, not only predicts that Neoptolemos and Philoktetes will take Troy but also warns that they must do it in the proper way: "with piety toward all things / relating to the gods."

914 *sleep will grip him soon* Note that the onset of sleep, unlike sleep itself, has a preemptive character. Neoptolemos
characterizes it as an *event*. This differs markedly from the
Chorus's softer-edged evocation of sleep as a beatific state
of being.

919–926 *Sweet sleep that feels . . . Come* Lullaby. Sleep identified as a healing agent.

923 *this most serene glow* The daughter of Asklepios, the god
of healing, is Aigla, the "gleam of serenity" that healing
brings.

930–932 *The Right Moment is . . . victory* A common saying.
It's not that they don't feel for Philoktetes, they do, but they
have a task to accomplish. N.B. Though the sailors serve
under Neoptolemos, they will on occasion question or
(obliquely) correct him. Unlike soldiers in modern military
structures, they have a complex historical relation to their
lord, including as retainers. They do not operate, as is the
norm now, within a relatively freestanding, codified chain
of command.

935 He's *the victory trophy* Neoptolemos must bring not only
the bow but Philoktetes himself back to Troy.

940 *sick men sleep sleepless, they pick up on things* Literal: "all
men's sleep is keen of sight in sickness" (Ussher, 39).

947–956 *But now, my boy, the wind . . . quickly, without
warning* As conceived in this translation, the Chorus is a
collectivity in which several voices, at times with individual
inflections, express common perspectives or concerns. e.g.,
the voice coming from the Chorus in 952 ("Strengthless he
is, like one laid at the edge of Hades") is different from that
of the practical-minded Leader. The same sententious voice

is heard in 195–197 ("Dark are the doings of the gods . . . short of their doom"). Not that these distinctions need be observed, but in contemporary (maskless) production they're available as a dramatic resource.

969–970 *you're / naturally noble* Belief in the efficacy of breeding, or bloodline, is a given.

1036 *you filthy piece of work!* Literal: "you contrivance of villainy" (Ussher, 142).

1093–1094 *You learned this / from truly evil teachers* Cf. Neoptolemos' words at 430–433.

1099–1101 *You won't get back / here and / give me* that bow? A negative future question posed as a command. The phrasing reflects a common Greek construction. The difficulty, in English, is in keeping it from sounding like a plea. It may help to deliver 1100–1101 in a heavy-footed way, hence the gaps between the last four words.

1116 *Let that man* drag *me off?* Emphasis to indicate that "drag" is literal, not metaphorical. Philoktetes will be forced, not led, away.

1119–1121 *ZEUS rules . . . I carry out his orders* That Odysseus is cynical doesn't preclude his having beliefs. "Odysseus— whatever his interpretation of it—is concerned to bring a prophecy, in which he believes, to fulfillment" (Ussher, 145).

1140–1142 *hands . . . now / together, held helpless* His hands are held down by the guards on either side of him.

1225 *The two of us* Neoptolemos speaking as though he and Odysseus were still of one mind in this mission.

1233–1234 *O forlorn space, all echoed up / reeking with my pain* The Greek mingles "both the groaning and the stench" (Webster, 136).

1372 *would you be so* kind *as to say* why Aggressive (faux) politeness.

1404 *You will be* Odysseus's line has been lost. "You will be" is the translator's interpolation.

1418 *But you, son of Poias* Removed, awkward phrasing. Neoptolemos is apprehensive, uncertain what reception he'll get.

1523 *And O my eyes* Literally, "orbs." In the remarkable phrase of T. B. L. Webster: "The lonely man's eyes have a life of their own . . ." (152).

1532–1534 *Men whose souls / have conceived, once . . . evils* Another *gnōmē*.

1562 *You, I should imagine* Neoptolemos "dismisses the question (with light irony) as one that cannot seriously be intended" (Ussher, 160).

1595–1596 *Not till you've heard / what I will say* As Herakles speaks from a cultural and historical context that is fundamental, and more comprehensive, than any contained within personal or otherwise partial perspectives, his word is authoritative.

1619 *spoils such as common soldiers get* See introduction (5).

1631ff. *Yet remember, when / you sack Troy show piety* Implicitly, though unmistakably, an admonition to Neoptolemos.

1669–1670 *the god . . . subduing everything* Zeus.

1673 *the nymphs of the sea* The Nereids, patrons of sailors and fishermen.

WORKS CITED AND CONSULTED

Aristotle. *Aristotle's Poetics*. Trans. Leon Golden. Tallahassee: Florida State University Press, 1981.

———. *The Art of Rhetoric*. Trans. John Henry Freese. Loeb Classical Library 193. Cambridge, MA: Harvard University Press, 1967.

Blundell, Mary Whitlock. *Helping Friends and Harming Enemies: A Study in Sophocles and Greek Ethics*. Cambridge: Cambridge University Press, 1989.

Boegehold, Alan L. *When a Gesture Was Expected*. Princeton, NJ: Princeton University Press, 1999.

Carpenter, Thomas H., and Christopher A. Faraone, eds. *Masks of Dionysus*. Ithaca, NY: Cornell University Press, 1993.

Cartledge, Paul. *Ancient Greek Political Thought in Practice*. Cambridge: Cambridge University Press, 2009.

Csapo, Eric. *Actors and Icons of the Ancient Theater*. Malden, MA: Blackwell-Wiley, 2010.

Csapo, Eric, and William J. Slater. *The Context of Ancient Drama*. Ann Arbor: University of Michigan Press, 1994.

Eagleton, Terry. *Sweet Violence: The Idea of the Tragic*. Malden, MA: Blackwell, 2003.

Easterling, P. E., ed. *The Cambridge Companion to Greek Tragedy*. Cambridge: Cambridge University Press, 1997.

Edmunds, Lowell. *Theatrical Space and Historical Place in Sophocles' "Oedipus at Colonus."* Lanham, MD: Rowman & Littlefield, 1996.

Else, Gerald F. *The Origin and Early Form of Greek Tragedy*. New York: Norton, 1965.

Foley, Helene P. *Female Acts in Greek Tragedy*. Princeton, NJ: Princeton University Press, 2001.

Garland, Robert. *The Greek Way of Death*. Ithaca, NY: Cornell University Press, 1985.

———. *The Greek Way of Life*. Ithaca, NY: Cornell University Press, 1990.

Goldhill, Simon. *Reading Greek Tragedy*. Cambridge: Cambridge University Press, 1986.

Gould, Thomas. *The Ancient Quarrel Between Poetry and Philosophy*. Princeton, NJ: Princeton University Press, 1990.

Grene, David, trans. *Philoctetes: The Complete Greek Tragedies*. Ed. David Grene and Richmond Lattimore. University of Chicago Press, 1957.

Guthrie, W. K. C. *The Greeks and Their Gods*. Boston: Beacon Press, 1950.

Hall, Edith. *Greek Tragedy: Suffering Under the Sun*. Oxford University Press, 2010.

Hammond, Paul. *The Strangeness of Tragedy*. Oxford University Press, 2009.

Hanson, Victor Davis. *A War Like No Other*. New York: Random House, 2005.

Herodotus. *The Landmark Herodotus: The Histories*. Ed. Robert B. Strassler. New York: Pantheon Books, 2007.

Hughes, Bettany. *The Hemlock Cup: Socrates, Athens and the Search for the Good Life*. New York: Knopf, 2010.

Jebb, R. C., trans. *Antigone*. By Sophocles. Cambridge: Cambridge University Press, 1928. (Originally published 1888.)

———, trans. *Ajax*. By Sophocles. Cambridge: Cambridge University, 1896.

———, trans. *Electra*. By Sophocles. Cambridge: Cambridge University, 1894.

———, trans. *Oedipus Coloneus*. By Sophocles. Cambridge: Cambridge University, 1886.

———, trans. *Philoctetes*. By Sophocles. Cambridge: Cambridge University, 1898.

———, trans. *Oedipus Tyrannus*. By Sophocles. Cambridge: Cambridge University, 1883.

———, trans. *Trachiniae*. By Sophocles. Cambridge: Cambridge University, 1892.

Kagan, Donald. *Pericles of Athens and the Birth of Democracy*. New York: Touchstone–Simon & Schuster, 1991.

Kirkwood, G. M. *A Study of Sophoclean Drama*. Cornell Studies in Classical Philology 31. Ithaca, NY: Cornell University Press, 1994.

Knox, Bernard M. W. *Essays: Ancient and Modern*. Baltimore: Johns Hopkins University Press, 1989.

———. *The Heroic Temper: Studies in Sophoclean Tragedy*. Berkeley: University of California Press, 1964.

Lefkowitz, Mary R. *The Lives of Greek Poets*. Baltimore: Johns Hopkins University Press, 1981.

Lloyd-Jones, Hugh, trans. *Ajax*. By Sophocles. Loeb Classical Library 20. Cambridge, MA: Harvard University Press, 1994.

————, trans. *Philoctetes*. By Sophocles. Loeb Classical Library 21. Cambridge, MA: Harvard University Press, 1994.

Lloyd-Jones, Hugh, and N. G. Wilson. *Sophoclea: Studies on the Text of Sophocles*. Oxford: Clarendon Press, 1990.

Logue, Christopher. *Patrocleia*. London: Villiers, Ltd. Scorpion Press, 1962.

Phillips, Carl, trans. Introduction and notes by Diskin Clay. *Philoctetes*. By Sophocles. New York: Oxford University Press, 2003.

Pickard-Cambridge, Arthur. *The Dramatic Festivals of Athens*. 2nd ed. Revised with a new supplement by John Gould and D. M. Lewis. Oxford: Clarendon Press, 1988.

Plutarch. *The Rise and Fall of Athens: Nine Greek Lives*. Trans. Ian Scott-Kilvert. London: Penguin, 1960.

Radice, Betty. *Who's Who in the Ancient World*. London: Penguin, 1971.

Rehm, Rush. *The Play of Space: Spatial Transformation in Greek Tragedy*. Princeton, NJ: Princeton University Press, 2002.

Reinhardt, Karl. *Sophocles*. New York: Barnes & Noble– Harper & Row, 1979.

Roisman, Hanna M. *Sophocles: Philoctetes*. London: Gerald Duckworth & Co., 2005.

Schein, Seth L., trans. Sophokles: *Philoktetes*. Focus Classical Library, 2003.

Seaford, Richard. *Reciprocity and Ritual: Homer and Tragedy in the Developing City-State*. Oxford: Clarendon Press, 1994.

Segal, Charles. *"Oedipus Tyrannus": Tragic Heroism and the Limits of Knowledge*. 2nd ed. New York: Oxford University Press, 2001.

————. *Sophocles' Tragic World: Divinity, Nature, Society.* Cambridge, MA: Harvard University Press, 1995.

————. *Tragedy and Civilization: An Interpretation of Sophocles.* Cambridge, MA: Harvard University Press, 1981.

Taplin, Oliver. *Greek Tragedy in Action.* Berkeley: University of California Press, 1978.

Thucydides. *The Landmark Thucydides: A Comprehensive Guide to the Peloponnesian War.* Ed. Robert B. Strassler. New York: Touchstone–Simon & Schuster, 1996.

Ussher, R. G., ed. and trans. *Philoctetes.* By Sophocles. Warminster, UK: Aris & Phillips, 1990.

Vernant, Jean-Pierre, ed. *The Greeks.* Trans. Charles Lambert and Teresa Lavender Fagan. Chicago: University of Chicago Press, 1995.

Vernant, Jean-Pierre, and Pierre Vidal-Naquet. *Myth and Tragedy in Ancient Greece.* Trans. Janet Lloyd. New York: Zone Books, 1990.

Webster, T. B. L., ed. *Philoctetes.* By Sophocles. Cambridge: Cambridge University Press, 1970.

Whitman, C. E. *Sophocles.* Cambridge, MA: Harvard University Press, 1951.

Wiles, David. *Greek Theatre Performances: An Introduction.* Cambridge: Cambridge University Press, 2000.

————. *Tragedy in Athens: Performance Space and Theatrical Meaning.* Cambridge: Cambridge University Press, 1997.

Winkler, John J., and Froma I. Zeitlin, eds. *Nothing to Do with Dionysos?: Athenian Drama in Its Social Context.* Princeton, NJ: Princeton University Press, 1990.

Winnington-Ingram, R. P. *Sophocles: An Interpretation*. Cambridge: Cambridge University Press, 1980.

Zimmern, Alfred. *The Greek Commonwealth: Politics and Economics in Fifth-Century Greece*. 5th ed. New York: Modern Library, 1931.

ACKNOWLEDGMENTS

Fifty years ago Christopher Logue's *Patrocleia* taught me something about the ancient Greeks. But that immensely slender book taught still more about the body English of format and typography—above all the urgency of writing, translating, with one's whole being and resources.

Ten years later, co-translating Aeschylus' *Prometheus Bound* with John Herington, I learned a comparable lesson: translation begins with the whole work, from its generative sources to the passionate arc of living matter that is brought into play. This doesn't mean slighting details, or playing fast and loose with words, but feeling through to their particularity: to what the words are doing, as well as to what they're saying.

ABOUT THE TRANSLATOR

Aided by a National Defense Fellowship, James Scully received his PhD (1964) from the University of Connecticut, where he later taught for many years. He has received a Lamont Poetry Award from the Academy of American Poets (1967) and Guggenheim, Ingram Merrill Foundation, and NEA fellowships, as well as translation awards and a Bookbuilders of Boston award for book cover design. He and the late C. John Herington co-translated Aeschylus' *Prometheus Bound*.

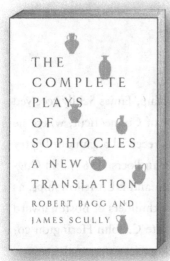
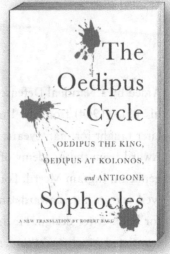

Printed in the USA
CPSIA information can be obtained
at www.ICGtesting.com
LVHW031133310824
789807LV00005B/176

9 780062 132161